British Rail Handbook

B.K.Cooper

LONDON

IAN ALLAN LTD

First published 1981
Reprinted 1981

ISBN 0 7110 1027 7

Published by Ian Allan Ltd, Shepperton, Surrey; and printed by Ian Allan Printing Ltd at their works at Coombelands in Runnymede, England

Addenda

Some announcements of forthcoming developments on BR were made after the Handbook had gone to press. They are shown below under the headings of the sections to which they apply.

Section 7: Electric Traction and Motive Power

British Rail is proposing to close $15\frac{3}{4}$ miles of the Woodhead Tunnel trans-Pennine route between Penistone and Hadfield, and to transfer the freight traffic to the Diggle and Hope Valley routes. The line between Hadfield, Glossop and Manchester with its emu passenger service would remain open.

Section 12: Freight Services and Rolling Stock

British Rail has announced its intention to end its C&D (collection and delivery) Rail Express Parcels services from 1 July 1981. The Red Star service is unaffected.

Contents

Preface 5
1 BR — A National Railway System 6
2 Numbering and Wheel Arrangement 13
3 Permanent Way 21
4 Diesel Traction 36
5 Generators and Motors 47
6 Diesel Locomotives and dmus 52
7 Electric Traction and Motive Power 77
8 The Air Brake 122
9 125mile/h and Above 127
10 Signalling 134
11 Passenger Rolling Stock 153
12 Freight Services and Rolling Stock 165

Fig 1 Principal routes of British Railways and of the railway system in Northern Ireland and the Irish Republic

Preface

A comparison of British Railways in the last days of steam with British Railways today mirrors the changes that have taken place throughout the industrial world. The process continues, and the observer of railways, as he reads of new developments, may sometimes sigh for simpler days when what one learned in one's youth was a solid and satisfactory foundation for understanding what came later. There were changes in shape, size and appearance, it is true. The first streamliners were a rude shock when they appeared and a referendum of enthusiasts would probably have shown a majority in favour of the classic Gresley Pacific outline rather than the impassive battlewagon contours of *Silver Link*. But the principles remained the same in motive power and other areas of operation. So did the function of the railways as 'common carriers' obliged to accept, albeit sometimes unwillingly in later years, anything from a trainload of temperance excursionists to a crate of whisky.

To keep pace with current developments there must be a solid foundation of understanding of the present scene on which to build. This handbook has been compiled with the purpose of providing it. As Editor, I have time and again been interested to discover how often railway 'facts' which have been lodged in the mind too long turn out on inspection to have been converted by time into little more than half-truths, and how much that we 'know' is only half understood. My sessions with British Railways officers who have helped me in compiling the sections for which I was responsible, and have patiently checked the text, have been illuminating. Railways are an expanding subject, ranging from trains to telecommunications, from minibuffets to microprocessors. Stand on a bridge and look down at the track, or on a station platform and look up at the catenary system. At once questions form in the mind. I hope this handbook, its contributors — learned or simply inquisitive — and the unfailing collaboration of the British Railways Press Office, have provided some of the answers.

1 BR — A National Railway System

The title 'British Railways' stems from the Transport Act of 1947. This measure, which came into effect on 1 January 1948, nationalised the railways, London Transport, the canals and the railway-owned docks, placing them all under the control of the British Transport Commission. A Railway Executive was formed as a central management for the railways, which were organised as five Regions: Eastern, London Midland, North Eastern, Scottish and Southern. The names, except for North Eastern, which was merged with the Eastern Region in 1967, remain today but there have been numerous adjustments of Regional boundaries since that time. There has also been much 'slimming' of the system by the closure of uneconomic lines, and the total of 11,020 route-miles in 1979 compared with some 20,000 route-miles at 1 January 1948.

Even before World War II the railways had suffered from competition for freight from road hauliers. The postwar world was to be much more intensively 'motorised' and although for the first few years private motoring was restricted by shortages of vehicles and fuel, once these difficulties passed it began to erode passenger traffic more seriously than ever before. From 1948 to 1952, however, the railways were able to show surpluses on their operation of freight and passenger trains but their new organisation did not operate as smoothly and efficiently as had been hoped, and by the Transport Act of 1953 the Railway Executive was abolished, more power and independence being given to the Regional managements, which now operated under Area Boards corresponding in some degree to the Boards of Directors of the previous companies.

The Commission now pressed the Regions to introduce lightweight diesel trains in place of stopping steam trains in many areas, following this with the launch in 1955 of its Plan for the Modernisation and Re-equipment of British Railways, in which the elimination of steam was stated as official policy. But the days of the BTC were numbered. The financial results of the railways were beginning to cause concern and the Government of the day commissioned an independent study of the organisation and efficiency of the Commission. On the basis of several reports from the investigators it decided that the BTC should go. It was abolished by the Transport Act of 1962, which set up the British Railways Board as from 1 January 1963 and replaced the previous Area Boards with Regional Boards. Certain accountancy measures were taken in the hope of establishing a base for the purely commercial operation of the railways in the future. The BRB's first Chairman was Dr Richard Beeching (later Lord Beeching), who had been appointed Chairman of the British Transport Commission in 1961.

Dr Beeching at once set on foot studies to decide the form the railway system should take and the policies under which it should be operated if it was to pay its way without subsidy from the public funds. Two reports were produced, the first (in 1963) called *The Re-shaping of British Railways,* and the second (in 1965) *The Development of the Major Trunk Routes*. The 'Re-shaping' report proposed withdrawing some 245 passenger train services and closing over 2,000 stations. In the second report the routes that were expected to carry the major traffic flows in the future were specified and it was shown that, where duplication existed, major economies could be achieved by concentrating traffic on one of them. The results are seen today in examples such as the concentration of London-Exeter-Plymouth traffic at Paddington, with the former Southern route to the West reduced to single track for much of the way beyond Salisbury. A still harsher fate befell the former Great Central main line to London Marylebone, which was closed as far as its services between London and the Midlands were concerned in 1966 although Marylebone remains open for trains to Aylesbury by the former Metropolitan & Great Central Joint route, and to Banbury by the former Great Western & Great Central Joint line via High Wycombe and the old Great Western 'direct' route to Birmingham via Bicester. Over the years the Manchester, Leeds and Anglo-Scottish trains from St Pancras have been withdrawn, leaving St Pancras to supply the London-Leicester-Nottingham-Sheffield services for which it was once in competition with the Great Central.

The procedure for closing lines as recommended in the Beeching reports provided for the hearing of objections and there were plenty of these, so that the process went on slowly if inexorably. A new

Government elected in 1964 did not subscribe to the view that British Railways could operate as a purely commercial undertaking and at the same time provide a satisfactory service to the public as a whole. After long discussion and consultation a new Transport Act became effective in 1968. It acknowledged that certain passenger services could not be economically viable but saw them as necessary on social grounds and so they would be supported by grants renewable from year to year as long as their retention could be justified. In certain provincial areas Passenger Transport Authorities were set up to promote the integration of local transport, with Passenger Transport Executives to manage the services. The PTEs were empowered to make arrangements with British Railways for providing train services coordinated with local public transport, and to support them with subsidies where necessary.

On the freight side the sundries business, which had long been uneconomical and unsatisfactory in speed of service, was handed over to National Carriers Limited, which also acquired the railways' road vehicles and the terminals where sundries traffic had been handled. A new company, Freightliners Limited, was formed to operate the 'liner train' container services which had been proposed in the Beeching documents and had been introduced from 1965 onwards.

The 1968 Act also allowed railway works to manufacture rolling stock and general engineering products for private customers. The BRB therefore set up a subsidiary company, British Rail Engineering Limited, to carry on this business. BREL came into being in January 1970. The new organisation was empowered to build for export and entered into partnership with the Birmingham company of Metro-Cammell, which embodied the marketing expertise and widespread overseas representation long associated with its internationally-known predecessor, the Metropolitan-Cammell Carriage & Wagon Co Ltd. The present partnership is known as BRE-Metro.

It had been intended that the grants to rail services under the 1968 Act should be progressively reduced, but operating deficits continued and in 1973 the Minister of Transport called upon BRB to make an exhaustive enquiry into the economics of railway working. It was now clearly shown that the railway system could not be self-supporting, that nothing was to be gained by cutting it further, and that the social benefit of keeping lines open outweighed the commercial loss. Although a General Election brought a change of government, these conclusions were accepted and embodied in the Transport Act of 1974. Under this Act the payments for individual passenger services authorised in 1968 were replaced by overall payments as necessary to enable BRB to fulfil its obligation to provide a public passenger service. BRB produces a budget each year showing an estimated total passenger revenue for the year ahead, plus a contribution from freight and parcels services and payments from Passenger Transport Executives for operating services on their behalf. The total is deducted from the estimated working expenditure, the remainder being the sum required from the Minister to make up the difference. This figure, originally described as 'compensation', is now regarded as the contract price for which BR undertakes to operate passenger services in order to fulfil its public service obligation.

An important measure affecting freight services introduced in Section 8 of the 1974 Act authorised grants to industry towards the cost of building private sidings and terminals. Many firms have taken advantage of this aid and substantial volumes of traffic have been transferred from road to rail, with benefit to the environment. Another development since that time has been the restoration to BRB of a controlling interest in Freightliners Limited, which took effect in August 1978.

Research

Many aspects of mechanical, electrical, electronic and civil engineering are involved in railway working today. In all these areas there is scope for development and innovation and the management of British Railways has always been alive to the need for research. A Chief Research Officer was appointed by the British Transport Commission in 1949, but the opportunity to centralise research activities did not come until the organisation had developed further. A research and development centre was set up at Derby in 1962. New laboratories were built and were formally opened in 1964. Around them the present Railway Technical Centre has grown. Here a staff of some 900 conducts work on track, vehicles, traction systems, braking, train control and signalling, and many associated subjects. The Centre is supported by six area laboratories dispersed over the system to handle day-to-day problems. Their work provides feedback which helps in shaping the research programme of the Technical Centre so that its work is of maximum benefit.

Experience from the laboratories is made available to other administrations all over the world by BR's subsidiary, Transmark, a worldwide consultancy service which has won Queen's Awards for Export Achievement.

Shipping and Hovercraft

In taking over the four railway groups in 1948 the British Transport Commission acquired their shipping fleets. These continued to be operated by the new Regions until 1969 when central management was introduced. The British Railways Board then formed a Shipping & International Services Division which is a member of the Sealink consortium in association with Belgian, Dutch and

Below: Sealink cross-Channel ship MV Hengist. Sealink

Right: Testing high-voltage insulators in artificial rain conditions at the BR Technical Centre, Derby. BR

French services. At the end of 1979 the Shipping Division owned 34 ships. Harbours, managed by the Division as a separate business, numbered 11. Since 1978 the International Services have been separated from Shipping, which has become Sealink UK Limited.

British Rail Hovercraft Ltd was inaugurated in 1966 with services between Southampton and Cowes. Services from Dover to Boulogne and Calais were introduced later in connection with rail services on both sides of the Channel.

Hotels and Catering

British Transport Hotels Ltd runs hotel, train catering and refreshment room services. There are now 29 hotels in the group, including five in London. One of the latter is the Grosvenor Hotel at Victoria, which returned to BTH in 1977 after some years of operation by another company under a management agreement. Travellers-Fare, the train catering and refreshment room side of BTH, was made a self-contained business division within the organisation in 1978.

Top: A Class 507 coach body undergoes resonance tests at the BR Technical Centre, Derby.
Above: HST passenger coaches during manufacture in the Litchurch Lane Works, Derby, of British Rail Engineering. BR

2 Numbering and Wheel Arrangement

by C. J. Leigh

The first diesel locomotives to enter service on British Railways were some shunters and a handful of largely experimental main line types which had been ordered by the railway companies prior to Nationalisation in 1948. Under the original BR numbering scheme, which was concerned mainly with steam locomotives, five-digit numbers were used and diesels were numbered in the 10000 series, electric locomotives from 20000, ex-Southern steam locomotives from 30000 and so on. Only the Western Region retained the former GWR system occupying the 1-9999 series.

The system for diesel locomotives was changed in the mid-1950s when new locomotives were ordered under the 1955 Modernisation Plan. In this scheme 'D' and 'E' prefixes were to be used to denote diesel or electric locomotives and numbering commenced with D1 through to D9999. Pre-Nationalisation diesels retained their previous numbers as most had only a short life expectancy. A system of power classification was also introduced at this time and this was to have used an alphabetical arrangement with the letter A denoting the lowest power range. However, before any new locomotives had been completed the system was changed to a numerical arrangement as shown below:

Type 1	Locomotives up to 1,000hp	D8000 series
Type 2	Locomotives between 1,000-1,500hp	D5000-D5999
Type 3	Locomotives between 1,500-1,999hp	D6000-D7999
Type 4	Locomotives of 2,000hp or more	D1-1999
Type 5	Added subsequently for locomotives of 3,000hp or more	D9000 series

The numbering scheme was to be tied to this classification by allocating blocks of numbers as shown, but by the mid-1960s this had been complicated by large deliveries of locomotives in some classes with the result that some were numbered out of sequence. The last Brush Type 4s to be built, for instance, were numbered

D1100-11 while the earlier members occupied the D1500-1999 bracket. By 1968 some non-standard classes were being withdrawn and this provided an opportunity for a revision of the numbering system to suit computer operation, the D prefixes having been abandoned when steam working ended in 1968.

Left and below left: Nameplates of Class 87 electric locomotives. N. E. Preedy

Bottom left: Class 45/0 diesel-electric No 45.055 was one of the locomotives of this class which were given names before the practice of naming was resumed on a wider scale in 1978. N. E. Preedy

Under the new system introduced in 1973, a five-digit number was employed, with the first two digits denoting the locomotive class and based on power rating, and the last three digits indicating the actual locomotive number. The class coding was now simplified so that the 10,000 series indicated shunting locomotives and main line locomotives under 1,000hp, the 20,000 series denoted 1,000hp-plus locomotives in the former Type 2 category, 30,000 series, Type 3 and so on. Under this scheme the English Electric Class 20 Bo-Bos moved into the Class 2 category. Apart from its suitability for computerisation, the new scheme offered a further advantage in that the third digit could be used to indicate a sub-class. Thus, for instance, Class 47 locomotives are shown as Class 47/0 for locomotives with steam heating equipment, Class 47/4 for locomotives with electric or dual-heating and Class 47/9 for the sole GEC-engine locomotive. At the time of writing some locomotives are being fitted with push-pull operating equipment and buck-eye couplers and renumbered in Class 47/7.

It is this scheme which is in current use, with diesel classes occupying the number series up to 56,000, dc electric locomotives from 70,000 and ac electrics from 81,000.

The naming of modern motive power seems to have been largely a question of regional policy and has been from the outset a rather haphazard one. The Western Region named all its original Type 4 diesel-hydraulics, and with only two exceptions these followed the 'Warship' theme. The final class of main line diesel-hydraulics was to have been named after West Country beauty spots, but in a final bid to assert itself the WR selected a batch of largely meaningless names, all with 'Western' prefixes. No Southern and few Scottish Region locomotives received names, and it was a long time before all 22 of the ER 'Deltics' received their names. The LMR began by fitting the names of famous ocean liners to its EE Type 4s but soon stopped, fitted 'Peak' plates to the first 10 of that class, and regiment names to some others and then gave up naming its locomotives.

The prospect of early withdrawal of its named hydraulics led the WR to name a few Class 47s after its early steam locomotives and famous engineers, but most of these plates were removed after a few years. However, the Stephenson Locomotive Society was given permission to name electric locomotive No 87.001 in 1976 and a revival of naming was announced in 1977 to coincide with the Silver Jubilee celebrations of HM the Queen. Members of Class 87 and Class 50 were selected, and most of these had their plates fitted during 1978. Subsequently further Class 47s on Eastern, Western and London Midland Regions have been named. Many Class 86/2 electric locomotives have also received nameplates, and in 1980 the Southern Region named four Class 33 diesels and a Class 73 electro-diesel.

A standard information panel is now applied to the cabside of most locomotives, and this is in the form of a white stencil as shown below:

Class	X
Weight tonnes Brake force tonnes ETH index RA Max speed mph	

The code A, V or X indicates air, vacuum or dual train braking. Class, weight (always in working order) and maximum speed are self-explanatory. The brake force is an indication of the locomotive's stopping power. It is shown in tons and calculated by a formula dependent on weight and certain other factors. All BR locomotives have a classification code which indicates their ability to carry concentrated weight (the lower the number, the lighter the weight). The RA (route availability) number is based on the weight per axle of the locomotive, and no locomotive may work over a route with a lower RA number than itself. Locomotives fitted with electric train heating equipment will also show an eth index on this panel, and this indicates the power output of the train heating equipment. Each coach has an eth rating, and the total of all the coach ratings in a train must not exceed the eth index figure on the locomotive.

The wheel arrangements of diesel shunting locomotives are shown by the Whyte system which was devised for steam locomotives. Currently only rigid framed four and six-wheel shunters are in use by BR and these are simply shown as 0-4-0 and 0-6-0. There are also some permanently coupled 'master and slave' units formed by pairs of modified 0-6-0s and these are shown as 0-6-0 + 0-6-0.

Main line diesel locomotives on BR are carried on four, six or eight-wheel bogies (the last-named consisting of a six-wheel bogie with a two-wheel pony truck pivoted within the main bogie frame). For these and for electric locomotives a different system of notation is used. It is based on the international system which counts axles instead of wheels, and it distinguishes between powered and non-

Below: Permanently-coupled pairs of diesel shunters for service at Tinsley yard form BR's only 0-6-0+0-6-0 class. Eric Bullen

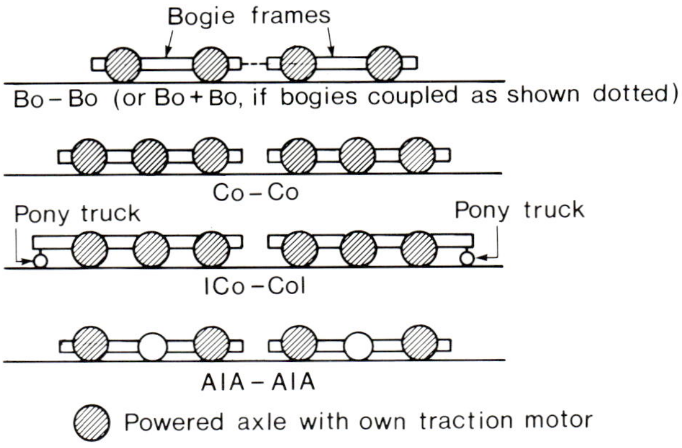

Fig 2 Wheel arrangements of British Railways electric and diesel-electric main line locomotives

powered or carrying axles. Powered axles are denoted by a letter (A, B or C according to whether there are one, two or three in the bogie), and carrying axles by a figure. Independently powered axles are shown by the suffix 'o'. Each bogie is shown separately with a hyphen between them. A locomotive with two bogies, both having two powered axles with a separate motor for each, is a Bo-Bo, three powered axles a Co-Co and so on. Individual drive is now so usual that the 'o' suffix is often omitted. In the Class 76 electric locomotives the bogies are coupled by an articulated joint that transmits tractive effort and the correct designation is Bo+Bo. This arrangement is obsolescent and the + sign is often omitted.

The numbering system employed for diesel and electric multiple units is more complex than that for locomotives, because not all Regions use the same system, and care must be taken not to confuse the different methods of numbering. Dealing first with dmus, each type is identified by a class number indicating its particular make and any detail differences are shown by a suffix number. These numbers fall in the series 100-99 for units with mechanical transmission and in the 200-299 series for units with electric tranmission. This information may be painted in small lettering on the inner ends of the vehicles but in order to distinguish individual cars a unique stock number, as used on the TOPS computer system, is painted on the side of the vehicle. This number follows the style of numbering used for coaching stock and consists of five digits preceded by the regional letter W, S, E, M or Sc depending on the Region to which the vehicle is allocated.

The Western and Southern Regions also use a unit number which will be found painted on the outer ends of the driving cars. On the WR this is preceded by an area code letter but units are often remarshalled and accordingly the unit number is generally disregarded by enthusiasts. On the Southern, however, the unit number is painted above the two-character headcode display on the cab ends, and is all-important as it is this, rather than individual coach numbers, which is used in identification. Consequently SR sets tend to remain in their fixed formations.

Similar differences affect the emu classes where anomalies are not confined to particular regions. On the LMR, older units and pre-Nationalisation designs are identified by their individual vehicle numbers, later units by a three-digit unit number and the most recent designs by a three-digit unit number preceded by the class number as on the first of the Advanced Passenger Train units, 370.001. Eastern and Scottish Regions follow a similar pattern but do not possess any early emu types. The Southern Region uses the same sytem as for its dmus, but new and refurbished units are being numbered in the standard BR six-digit system.

The six figure unit numbers have also been employed for IC125 units in the 253.XXX and 254.XXX series but since the power cars carrying these numbers are frequently remarshalled into different units the individual carriage stock numbers are the only reliable identification.

Locomotives no longer carry the four-digit descriptions of the train they are working. When this practice ceased the panels on which the descriptions had been displayed were blanked out but two circular apertures were left for showing white marker lights. This was an interim arrangement, but the standard system will be similar, consisting of two white lights at each end of the locomotive. For a time new locomotives were fitted with white and red marker lights in units with lenses of both colours, but this practice is being discontinued and a separate tail lamp must be carried when a locomotive is running light, and must be illuminated at night. In locomotives which still have the combined units, the red lights must be illuminated both by day and night during light running.

Headlights positioned on the vertical centre line at each end of the locomotive are being provided to allow staff working on the lineside to observe the approach of a locomotive at a greater distance. Although the purpose of the headlight is not to illuminate the track ahead, it does in practice assist the viewing of speed restriction cutouts, neutral section indicators and other signs.

Headlights and marker lights are being fitted to all new builds, and headlights are being fitted also to existing stock for working the higher speed services. Marker lights are to be fitted to all existing traction stock with a long life expectancy. In certain instances illuminated route indicators are being retained on electric multiple-unit stock for essential route indication purposes.

Below: Red and white marker light units and central headlamp on a Class 56 locomotive. BR

3 Permanent Way

by P. J. Coster

Rails

The rails used on BR in plain line or switches and crossings (s&c) are either flat-bottomed (FB) or bullhead (BH) in section, classified by their weights (lb) per yard length.

The BR standard rail is the 113lb FB rail, Type 113A, and except in s&c or where heavy curvature or a high incidence of wear obtains, it is used as continuously welded rail (cwr). Bullhead rail is now only used on BR in special circumstances such as on heavy curves, but it is still used extensively by London Transport. Both rail sections are shown in Fig 3. Many obsolete rail sections, both FB and BH, are still in use on BR, but as renewal falls due they will disappear. Those sections commonly in use today are listed below with their general area of use:

Types of rail in use on BR

Rail section	*Weight (lb/yd)*	*(kg/m)*	*Use*
FB			
113A*	113	56.1	Main lines, s&c and plain line cwr.
110A	110	54.6	As 113A but now gradually being replaced.
109	109	54.1	As 113A but was replaced by 110A in part, now by 113A.
98	98	48.6	Obsolete: only used as serviceable plain line cwr on secondary routes.
BM			
95†	95	47.1	As check rail on heavy curves. Was used for s&c in major layouts but has largely been replaced by 113A or 110A. Used on LT.

Note: Sections above are only available as serviceable rail except * (available new) and † (available new in limited quantities).

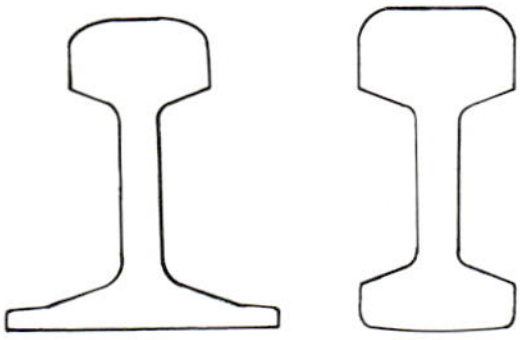

Fig 3 Flat bottom and Bullhead rail sections

Rails are supplied in lengths of 60ft (18.29m) and either used as such or depot-welded into lengths of 600-900ft (183-275m). Secondhand or 'serviceable' rails are cropped to removed the drilled ends, and then depot welded into similar lengths for use on secondary lines.

The track gauge is 1.432m (4ft 8.375in) except in existing jointed track 'inclined' and s&c predating 1966, where it is 1,435mm (4ft 8.5in).

Sleepers and Timbers

Sleepers are of concrete, hardwood or softwood, and are used under Plain line; their counterparts for s&c are described as 'timbers'. S&c timbers were of softwood, but many main line layouts have been renewed on hardwood in the last 10-15 years. Timbers are 12in×6in (305mm × 152mm) in section whereas wood sleepers are 10in × 5in (254mm × 127mm).

The standard sleeper is of prestressed concrete, and has evolved through a number of designs. Originally reinforced concrete sleepers were introduced in the 1930-40s, surviving, generally, longer on branch and secondary lines. The prestressed concrete sleeper was developed as a technically and economically feasible proposition in the 1950s and its development, with a view to eliminating the use of baseplates, was accelerated by the installation of cwr in the late 1950s and 1960s. Today, concrete sleepers are considerably cheaper than timber, and are used at every opportunity. They exist in many design forms, but new concrete sleepers are available today with a choice of two depths, a choice of length for the presence or otherwise of conductor rail, and for particular locations which require a check rail (on the inside of a sharp curve) or a rail joint.

Hardwood sleepers are of jarrah, and in contrast to the concrete sleeper with its Pandrol housings integrally cast, the attachment of two baseplates to each sleeper is required. New softwood sleepers are rarely used, only in very particular circumstances where their lower weight gives them the advantage over hardwood or concrete. There are of course many miles of softwood sleepered track still extant on BR, especially on secondary routes. The life of softwood sleepers varies according to use and standard of maintenance, but it is limited by decay to between 12 and 25 years: hardwood is expected to last over 30 years and some trial sections laid in the 1920-30 period have achieved nearly 40 years. Concrete is expected to last 50 years, and may, in fact, last longer.

Concrete bearers have been used in place of s&c timbers, but only in a few locations on an experimental basis. Another experiment currently being evaluated is the use of steel sleepers on plain line; although steel sleepers have been used at intervals over the years, the practice has not been convincingly successful. However, the cost of imported softwood may now be such as to make steel sleepers economically attractive.

Fastenings

The purpose of track fastening is to hold together rails and sleepers/timbers, with or without baseplates. Timbers and wood sleepers require baseplates for FB rail and chairs for BH, whilst concrete sleepers are designed for direct fastening, with a resilient pad between rail and sleeper for FB rail only.

The fastening currently used on BR is the Pandrol rail clip, located in a malleable iron housing cast into concrete sleepers, or in a cast iron baseplate on timbers/wood sleepers. Types of FB fastenings used earlier were either resilient or screwed, and many miles of plain tracks have earlier obsolete fastenings still in use. In the mid-1960s the BR standard s&c design was altered from 'inclined' to 'vertical': that is to say, whereas formerly each rail was inclined towards the other at 1 in 20 (to the vertical), with the new design each rail is vertical. The new design allowed a huge reduction in baseplate sizes and the incorporation of the Pandrol fastening in place of the earlier screw and clip fastening.

Switches and Crossings

The design of s&c layouts is built up using three units — the switch,

Above: Switches and crossings at Harpenden Junction, LMR (view taken before electrification). BR

common crossing and obtuse crossing. The switches are normally in pairs, left or right hand, and are available in eight sizes, A-F, Short G, and G. An A switch has a relatively sharp angle of divergence and the blade planing is short, while conversely a G switch has a fine angle of divergence and lengthy blade planing.

Common crossings were originally an assembly of two wing rails and a planed vee (consisting of a point rail and splice rail) bolted or pinned together with distance blocks. On heavily used routes the use of the 'built-up' or 'rolled' crossing has been reduced by the introduction of cast manganese steel crossings or welded versions of the 'rolled' crossing, with the introduction of vertical s&c.

Obtuse crossings are similar in appearance but their function is different. They are also a built-up unit which has been displaced partly by switch diamonds, and partly by cast manganese steel obtuse crossings.

A development of the common crossing in recent years, for use in high speed routes, is the swing nose crossing. Each unit and its variants are illustrated in Fig 4. Both types of crossing are classified on the angle of intersection of the gauge faces measured digitally, eg 1 in 8 (7° 9′ 9″). While rolled crossings can be manufactured to

Fig 4 Types of crossing

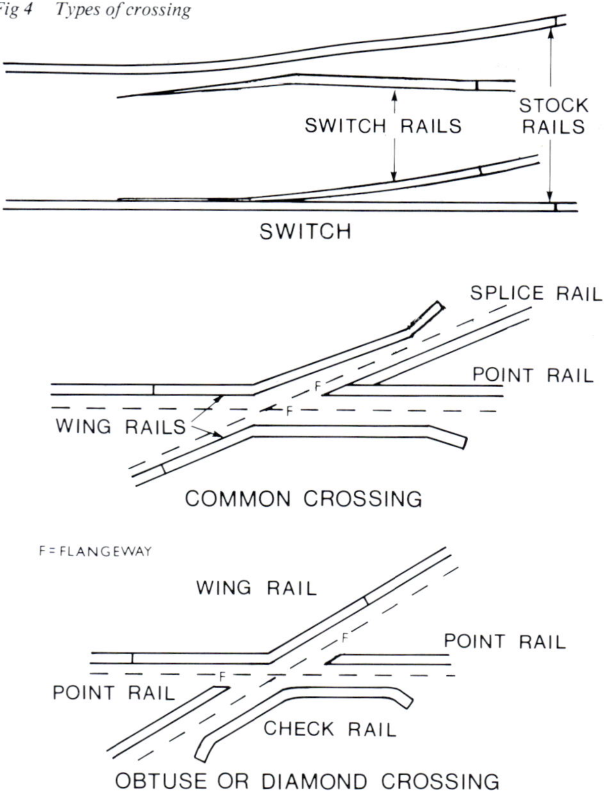

Fig 5 Combinations of switches and crossings

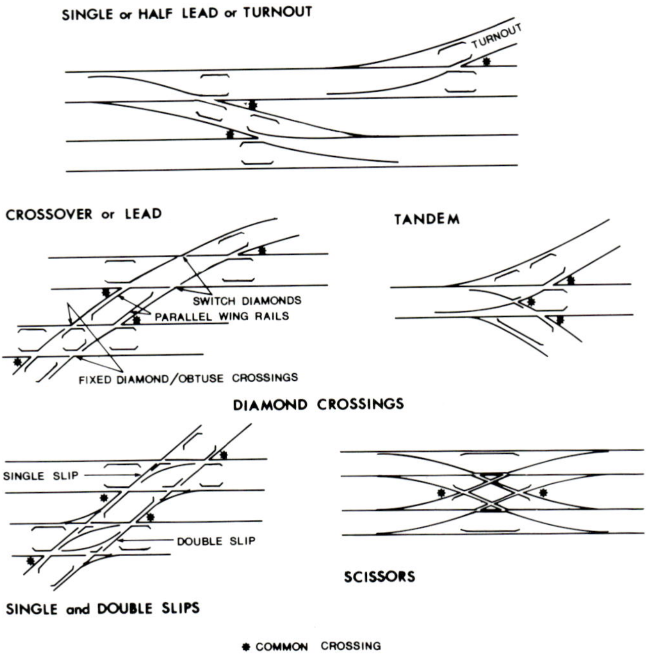

more or less any angle from 1 in 4 to $10\frac{3}{4}$, cast and welded crossings are available only in specific sizes (eg 1 in 7, $9\frac{1}{4}$, 1 in 28, 13, 15, $18\frac{1}{2}$, 21, 24 and 28).

Combinations of switches and crossings give the track configurations shown in Fig 5.

Reference to s&c layouts and single leads (Fig 6) is made by describing the switch and crossing configurations; for example a

Fig 6 Types of single lead

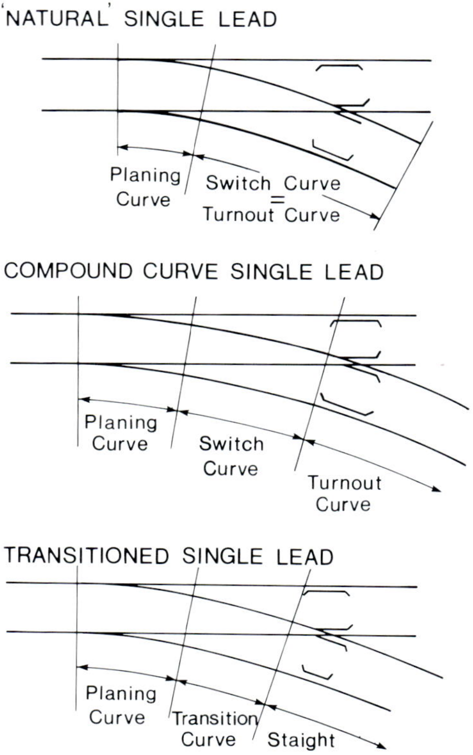

Bv8 single lead has a pair of vertical B switches and a 1 in 8 common crossing. Certain combinations of switches and crossing align to a circular curve in which the switch and turnout curves are the same. Geometry may require a combination in which the two curves are different, such as a Bv10$\frac{3}{4}$ single lead for example. The 'v' indicates a vertical design as distinct from the earlier 'inclined' designs.

The use of single leads and crossovers in modern layouts has led to the development of transitioned designs which permit a smooth passage at speed through crossovers. The permitted speeds over single lead divergences and crossovers are given below:

Types of single-lead crossover used on BR

Type of switch	*Crossing angle (1 in —)*	*Radius of turnout curve (m)*	*Maximum permitted speed (mile/h, km/h)*	
			Single lead	*Crossover*
Av	7	141	20/35	15/30
Av	9.25	*	20/35	—
Bv	8	184	20/35	20/35
Bv	10.75	*	20/35	20/35
Cv	9.25	246	25/40	20/35
Cv	13	*	25/40	20/35
Dv	10.75	332	30/50	—
Dv	15	*	30/50	30/50
Ev	15	645	40/70	—
Ev	21	*	40/70	40/70
Fv	18.5	981	50/85	—
Fv	28	*	50/85	50/85
SGv†	21	1264	60/100	—
SGv†	28	*	60/100	60/100
Gv	24	1650	70/115	—
Gv	28	*	70/115	70/115

* Curvature varies, and a transition curve is included in the turnout alignment

† SGv — Short Gv switches

Above: A Hull-Manchester dmu passes a 'ladder' crossing at Wincobank Junction. T. Dodgson

Track Alignment

Railway track alignment consists of a succession of straight and curved sections of various radii, and each change of radius requires a transition curve to allow the train to negotiate the change at its line speed in complete safety and at the acceptable standards of passenger comfort laid down.

A circular curve requires the track to be canted to avoid excessive centrifugal forces on the track and hence both unnecessarily high maintenance costs and passenger discomfort. The cant is designed to achieve the optimum situation, insofar as maintenance costs and riding standards are concerned, for the maximum train speed; the design or equilibrium speed of a curve is usually below the maximum permitted, so that at the former speed a cant deficiency exists. Cant deficiency is carefully controlled by the designer and a maximum value of 110mm is allowed. Actual cant may not normally exceed 150mm, ie the maximum theoretical cant permissible is 260mm. Theoretical cant values can only be developed at maximum rates for given speed levels (measured as a gradient, eg 1 in 600) and it is often this parameter which limits train speeds rather than theoretical cant values.

Above: Preparing the new layout at Marshgate Junction, south of Doncaster on the East Coast main line, in March 1979, showing lines to Humberside curving away to the right, the ECML running straight ahead, and the new lines to West Yorkshire in their early stages on the left. BR

Formation

The track structure of rails, fastenings, and sleepers is supported by a bed of consolidated ballast desirably 300-400mm deep. The original ground beneath usually is inadequate to support the imposed loads without natural or constructed drainage and some strengthening at the time of construction. Where the ground beneath is soft, eg clay, alluvium, a 'blanket' layer of granular material (eg sand or stone dust) is provided to allow water to drain away and to prevent the water-softened ground from working up into the ballast. In the latter circumstances the ability of the formation to withstand the impacts of wheel loads is reduced and the quality of track level and, to a degree, alignment, will deteriorate. The remedial treatment is hand reballasting and drainage improvement, in the short term, and formation renewal in the long term.

Ballast is usually crushed rock of high strength and attrition value which does not break or erode under traffic conditions; although the ready availability of limestone has led to its use as ballast on a wide scale in the past, in recent years the use of igneous, metamorphic, or hard sedimentary rocks (eg granite, dolerite, whinstone, gritstone) has spread to most of the major routes.

The purpose of track ballasting is to spread the load imposed by passing trains on the track over as large an area of ground as possible, so that the track neither suffers permanent deformation nor excessive downward deflection. The nature of ballast is such that the track alignment can be easily restored by manual or mechanical adjustment or fettling. With the introduction of cwr, particularly in association with concrete sleepers, the role of ballasting extended to include that of track stabilisation. The 'shoulder' of ballast beyond the sleeper ends is of particular importance in resisting lateral distortion or buckling in hot weather, and for cwr the shoulders are considerably wider than with the previous jointed track.

Permanent Way Maintenance

This subject comprises an enormous variety of tasks and is obviously of crucial importance, but may be classified under three broad headings: Manual maintenance, including inspection; Mechanised maintenance by on-track machines; and Relaying, reballasting and earthworks.

Manual Maintenance

The regular inspection of permanent way provides both a monitor on track safety and a fault reporting service. The need to repair or fettle the track is met either by use of a machine or by allocating staff to carry out repairs. Machines will realign track and restore longitudinal and cross levels to design values (tamping/lining machines), remove excess ballast and eliminate deficiencies (ballast

Below: Mechanised track maintenance equipment passes Victoria Park, Bristol. P. J. Fowler

regulator, and ballast train if required) or consolidate ballast (consolidator). Defective components can be replaced with the assistance of cranes or special motor trolleys with hydraulic lifting arms. Drainage work, hand reballasting, lubrication of switches, oiling fishplates and adjusting expansion gaps, and a whole host of other tasks remain as manual maintenance.

Mechanical Maintenance

Tamping, lining and consolidation are mechanical functions, which were previously executed by two or three machines: tamper, liner and, in some circumstances a consolidator. The modern 07 Plasser machines on BR combine all three functions.

Track levels are assessed relatively by the machine and the actual cant is compared with the design value. The tamper lifts the rails to the correct position and consolidates ballast very tightly beneath the sleepers by the action of its tines, which both vibrate and compress the ballast. Ahead of the tamping bank in the machine are the sluing jacks, which adjust the track laterally.

Track curvature is assessed by measuring the versines of the track over a short chord, at the end of which are the sluing jacks, and a long chord. If the short chord versine is not compatible with the long, then the sluing jacks adjust the versine until compatibility is achieved.

Below: Tamping and lining machine. BR

Above: A ballast regulator and track lifting and slewing machine at work at Druimuachdar Summit on the Perth-Inverness line. BR

Both track levels and alignment can be adjusted to new design values by machine if desired rather than simply smoothing out irregularities. 07 machines adapted for tamping and lining s&c are also in use, the principal difference being that the tamping banks can be traversed outwards or inwards and angled downwards, to work within the restricted clearances between rails.

Following the disturbance to the track during tamping and lining, the loosened ballast around the sleeper (and not beneath) must be reconsolidated by the machine to restore lateral stability.

Ballast regulators are machines which profile the track ballast, sweep up the surplus and release from a storage hopper where ballasting is deficient. They do not operate yet on conductor rail track.

Relaying, Reballasting and Earthworks

Track relaying and formation renovation are carried out with tracks under possession, with geographical limits and possession times clearly defined. Relaying is accomplished by the use of specialised twin jib cranes to exchange new 60ft track panels for old. After the new track is levelled and aligned the welded rails are substituted for the 'service' rails in the new track, usually one week later, and site-welded into the existing track.

Reballasting is usually carried out along with relaying, and is achieved by use of the ballast cleaner. The latter is a machine which has an endless cutting chain passing beneath the sleepers, removing the dirty ballast and conveying it up to where it is released, to pass over a series of vibrating screens. The good stone is returned to the track, and the accumulated dirt is discharged either to a spoil train or to the lineside. Fresh ballast is then unloaded to make good the loss in volume.

Formation renewal is simply the excavation of failed formation and its replacement. The drainage system is usually replaced during the operation as well. However, the volume of materials involved and the commitment in terms of men, machines and rolling stock is so large that formation renewal is a major weekend operation. The excavation is usually executed by hired hydraulic excavators.

S&c relaying is a more complicated operation for, while the extent of associated reballasting and formation renewal is less than for plain line, the achievement of a correct alignment and level through a layout is vitally important but harder to achieve than with plain line. It is common practice to rectify formation deficiencies first and undertake relaying as a subsequent operation.

The layout is preassembled, checked and then marked up for reassembly in situ, and carefully loaded in reverse order. On site, one or two rail cranes are used to lift out sections of s&c and either to replace them following formation work, or to lay in the new material. The relaid s&c is fettled and lifted to final level, and, where possible and desirable, rail joints are site-welded.

Above right: Relaying on the Western Region in readiness for HST services. The old track in the foreground has been removed and polythene sheeting laid to prevent soggy clay pumping up into the new ballast during the passage of trains. BR

Below: Complicated trackwork is often assembled at a pw depot before being dismantled and taken to site. This view shows the Waterloo West crossings laid out at Redbridge, Hants, before being transported to Waterloo and reassembled. BR

Future Development

Future requirements of the permanent way are likely to arise from increased traffic density and higher train speeds. In isolated cases there may be a demand for a higher axle load than the present 25tonne limit but in general terms the permanent way engineer will be concerned to prevent the costly track infrastructure from being impaired.

Some routes are up to the 125mile/h standards of alignment, and others will follow. Where train speeds above 125mile/h are proposed for the APT no special track improvements are required. On other routes a steady progress will be made towards higher speed limits of 90-125mile/h.

Experience with high speeds in Western Europe suggests that ballasted track will be able to cope with speeds up to 300mile/h or more. The paved concrete track developed by BR has not been widely used; the very high first cost of paved track, deriving from high materials costs and enormous disruption of traffic patterns, coupled with marginal savings in comparison with good ballasted track, make it only a viable proposition in places where particularly intractable engineering difficulties exist. It has been used successfully in several tunnels and between cutting retaining walls so far in BR and this is probably the only context in which it will be used in the next 10-20 years at least.

4 Diesel Traction

by Roger Ford

The Diesel Engine

While all internal combustion piston engines share the common operating sequence of induction, compression, ignition, power stroke and exhaust, the diesel engine differs from the more common petrol engine in one significant respect. In the petrol engine (or Otto cycle) the mixture of fuel and air is electrically ignited just before the piston reaches top dead centre on the compression stroke. Combustion is virtually instantaneous and takes place at almost constant volume. In the diesel cycle only air is induced into the cylinders and is then compressed. At maximum compression, the fuel is then sprayed into the cylinder through an injector and ignites spontaneously, due to the high temperature of the compressed air, and effectively burns at constant pressure.

The ratio of the volume of the cylinder with the piston at bottom dead centre to the volume with the piston at top dead centre is called the compression ratio. This ratio is an important factor in determining the thermal efficiency of an internal combustion engine — the amount of energy in the fuel which the engine turns into useful work. The higher the compression ratio, the higher the thermal efficiency. The compression ratio of a petrol engine is limited to single figures in practical terms because, at higher ratios, the heat caused by compression would cause the fuel to ignite too early, causing knocking and ultimately damage to the engine. The opposite is the case with the diesel engine where the compression ratio must not be below about 11:1 to ensure satisfactory cold starting. Thus, because of its higher compression ratio, the diesel engine is the most thermally-efficient internal combustion engine (including gas turbines). However, to withstand the higher stresses due to the high compression ratio the diesel engine has to be stronger than a petrol engine and thus weighs more for a given power output.

Diesel engines can be either four-stroke or two-stroke designs. In the four-stroke engine, the cycle takes place over four strokes of the piston ie up, down, up, down. If the first up stroke is taken as the exhaust stroke, the sequence (illustrated in Fig 7) is as follows:

Fig 7 The four-stroke diesel cycle

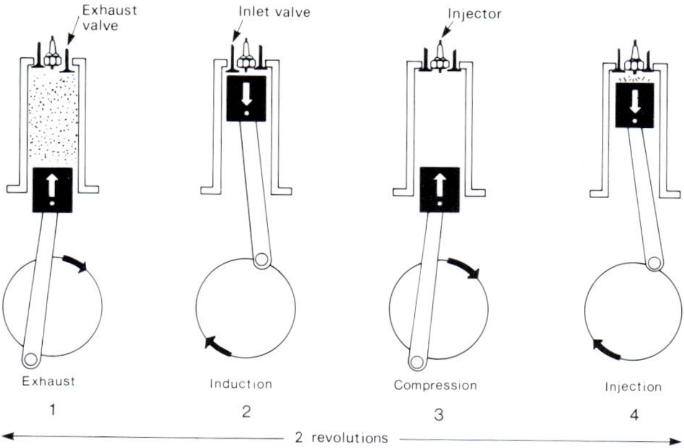

(1) On the up stroke, the combustion gases from the previous cycle are expelled through the exhaust valve.
(2) On the down stroke fresh air is drawn in through the inlet valve.
(3) The up stroke compresses the air in the cylinder.
(4) Fuel is injected and burns, driving the piston down.

The two stroke engine combines this sequence in one up and one down stroke as follows: starting with combustion:

(1) The piston is driven down by the pressure of combustion. At the end of this stroke ports in the cylinder walls are exposed which first let out the exhaust gases and then admit a fresh charge of air.
(2) The up stroke then compresses the air and ignition takes place when the fuel is injected, starting the cycle again.

As a two-stroke engine has a power stroke from each piston for each rotation of the crankshaft, compared with every other rotation for a four-stroke engine, it should theoretically give twice as much power. In fact, due to less efficient scavenging of the exhaust gases

Above: The 16-cylinder vee type diesel engine of a BR Class 56 freight locomotive. BR

and the reduced period over which fresh air can enter the cylinder the advantage is less.

The power obtained from a diesel engine depends on two factors: the amount of fuel which can be burnt in each combustion stroke and the number of combustion strokes per minute. The first factor depends on the volume of air in the cylinder — the more air, the more fuel can be burnt. The second factor depends on the rotational speed at which the engine runs and the number of cylinders. These are related because larger cylinders increase a number of critical parameters such as inertia forces and piston speeds. Thus for the same power output a designer could produce a large, slow-running engine or a smaller, lighter, fast-running engine with more cylinders.

The volume of air in the cylinder of an engine where the air is simply drawn in on the down stroke is fixed. Such an engine is called naturally aspirated. However, if more air could be drawn in, more fuel could be burned and more power produced without increasing the number of cylinders or the speed of rotation. This is achieved by supercharging, where the air is compressed and supplied to the engine under pressure. While compressors with mechanical drive have been used, the turbo-charger is universally used on British Rail's four-stroke diesel engine. The turbo-charger has a turbine, driven by the exhaust gases of the engine, on a common shaft with a centrifugal compressor. The advantage of the turbo-charger is that it automatically matches the volume of air supplied to the power required. As more fuel is supplied to the cylinders, a greater volume of exhaust gas is produced. This drives the turbine faster which in turn enables the compressor to supply more air to the engine, allowing more fuel to be burnt. Modern turbo-chargers provide air pressures up to around three times atmospheric pressure.

However, when air is compressed it becomes hotter which reduces its density. At high turbo-charger pressure-ratios this would reduce the efficiency of the engine as well as reducing the cooling effect of the charge air entering the cylinders. To overcome this the air is cooled after leaving the compressor and before entering the cylinder. This is achieved by passing the air through a heat exchanger where it heats up water — the reverse of an engine radiator. The heat exchanger is called an intercooler. Thus, traction diesel engines are offered in three forms: naturally aspirated, turbo-charged, and turbocharged and intercooled, although naturally aspirated units are rare nowadays when high power levels are generally required. The effect of intercooling can be seen in the rating of the Ruston-Paxman 16-cylinder engine used in the BR Class 56 freight locomotive. This is rated at 3,520hp with intercooling but 2,800hp when simply turbocharged.

The rating of a diesel engine is determined when it is built and depends on the speed of rotation, the degree of turbo-charging, whether intercooling is fitted, the life between overhauls required and the cylinder pressure. Thus an engine can have several ratings depending on duty. For example an engine for military use, where a high power-to-weight ratio is essential, can be set to give more power than the same design in a civil application. However, the military engine will be more highly stressed and will run for less time before requiring an overhaul. In the case of the Paxman Valenta 12-cylinder used in the Class 253/254 High Speed Trains, the traction rating is 2,250hp. However, the manufacturers quote its maximum output at 2,700hp, while for continuous industrial duty it is rated at 2,025hp.

The rating of different designs of engines can be compared in several ways. One indicator is the brake mean effective pressure (bmep), which is the average pressure in the cylinders required to produce the rated horsepower. This has grown steadily over the years. The

English Electric 16SVT engine, which powered the SR prototype locomotives 10201/3, had a bmep of 108lb/sq in. The Mk II version used in the BR Class 40 at 2,000hp had a bmep of 123.5lb/sq in. With the addition of intercooling, the same engine, now rated at 2,700hp in the Class 50 units, had a bmep of 167lb/sq in while in the 3,520hp Mk III version in the Class 56 this has risen to 217.5lb/sq in. Over the same period, the engine speed has risen from 750rev/min to 900rev/min. Rating can also be expressed as specific weight or lb/hp. The more highly rated the engine, the lower the specific weight. In the case of the English Electric V16 engine, the 16SVT of 1948 had a specific weight of 24lb/hp while the 1978 version reduced this to 14.9lb/hp. This would not be regarded as a highly rated engine and does not need to be, as light weight is not a requirement of a heavy freight locomotive. However, weight is of critical importance in the High Speed Train power car and the Paxman 12LC Valenta is an example of the highly rated modern traction diesel. This has a bmep of 272lb/sq in when rated at 2,250hp at 1,500rev/min and a specific weight of 6.8lb/hp. This specific weight is comparable with that of the complex ultra-lightweight Napier Deltic two-stroke diesel engine which was required to make the 3,300hp Class 55 locomotives possible in 1955.

While an engine's rating is pre-determined, it can be changed. It is rare for engine power to be increased for a number of reasons, including the lack of extra capacity in the electrical equipment and the fact that the governor, turbocharger and fuel injection system have been optimised at the stated output. However, engines have been de-rated on occasion. One example is the engine in the Class 56 locomotive. The manufacturer's rating, as given above, is 3,520hp. However, for the Class 56 it is rated at 3,250hp, partly to ensure high reliability and also because this is adequate for the duty. Another example is the Sulzer 12LDA 28C in the Class 47 locomotives. Initially the engine was rated at 2,750hp at 800rev/min. However, to reduce stresses caused by the out-of-balance forces set up by the pistons and crankshafts, the rotational speed was reduced to 750rev/min which de-rated the engine to 2,580hp.

Right: Engine-generator installation in a BRCW Class 26 locomotive. The load regulator is seen mounted on the generator, its dial indicating the position of the moving contact arm inside. The governor is behind it, but not visible, although the link and crank connection with the fuel rack can be seen. Ian Allan Library

Transmission

All British Rail main line diesel locomotives have electric transmission. So too have the High Speed Train and the Southern Region diesel multiple-units. Other diesel multiple-units have mechanical transmission.

In electric transmission, the diesel engine is coupled to a generator (direct current) or alternator (alternating current). Only the latest designs have alternators. The current generated is used to power the traction motors, which are dc machines. In locomotives with alternators, therefore, the motors are fed through rectifiers. These motors have the field windings in series with the armature windings. Series winding produces a torque/speed characteristic which is particularly suitable for rail traction in that as speed reduces — for example when the locomotive encounters an up grade — the torque increases.

General practice is for pairs of traction motors to be connected in series and the pairs connected in parallel. A characteristic of the dc traction motor is that as its rotational speed increases it generates a voltage which opposes that of its power supply (back emf). This voltage rises with speed, progressively reducing the voltage across the motor. This is countered by increasing the excitation of the main generator, which increases the output voltage as the current taken by the motors reduces. However, there is a limit to the excitation of the main generator field and, theoretically, the point could be reached where the back emf equalled the generator voltage and current ceased to flow. To prevent this, the characteristics of the traction motors are altered by weakening the excitation of their fields when the generator is at maximum excitation. This is achieved by inserting a resistance in the field circuit of each traction motor. This is known as field weakening or, because the resistance is shunted across the field coils in parallel, field diversion. With the fields weakened, the excitation of the generator can be reduced because the back emf from the motors has been reduced. As speed continues to increase, however, the traction motors follow the new characteristic curve and generator excitation is increased again to its maximum. The point at which field-weakening is introduced is called the 'unloading point' because if the motors continued running at their full-field characteristic the product of volts and amperes (ie the electrical power) would be less than the power being developed by the engine. Tractive effort and speed would fall. At this point the next stage of field weakening is introduced.

The number of stages of field weakening required depends on the motor and generator characteristics and the duties of the locomotive. Early BR diesels for mixed traffic duties had up to five or six stages. On later designs such as the Class 47 this was reduced to three weak field stages. The 'Deltic' locomotives with two diesel engines and two generators can produce a much higher voltage and only two stages of field weakening are needed to cover a speed range up to 100mile/h. With the introduction of the brushless alternator, the limitations on the main generator voltage, imposed by the commutator and brushes of the dc machine, were eliminated. Thus where the Class 47 dc generator is rated at 423V, 4,260A, the main alternator for the Class 56 has a continuous rating of 1,520V, 1,520A. With this higher voltage, only one stage of field weakening is necessary for an 80mile/h top speed. With the latest alternator drive in the High Speed Trains field weakening is not necessary at all.

Control

Electric transmission enables the full power of the diesel engine to be applied throughout the speed range of the locomotive. However this is not such a straightforward process as it sounds because the characteristics of the generator and the diesel engine differ. Fig 8 shows the characteristic curve of generator volts against generator current, with the speed of rotation of the generator constant. The second curve on the graph shows the constant power line which represents the output of a diesel engine. If the engine and generator set were coupled directly to the traction motors, it can be seen that at low generator voltages, ie when the locomotive was starting from rest, the power from the engine could overload the generator. However, as the excitation was increased, and the lower cross-over point of the two curves was passed the electrical load on the generator would exceed the power output of the diesel engine. Thus a control system is needed to match the generator characteristics to the power curve of the diesel engine. This is done electro-

Fig 8 Diesel engine and electric generator power curves

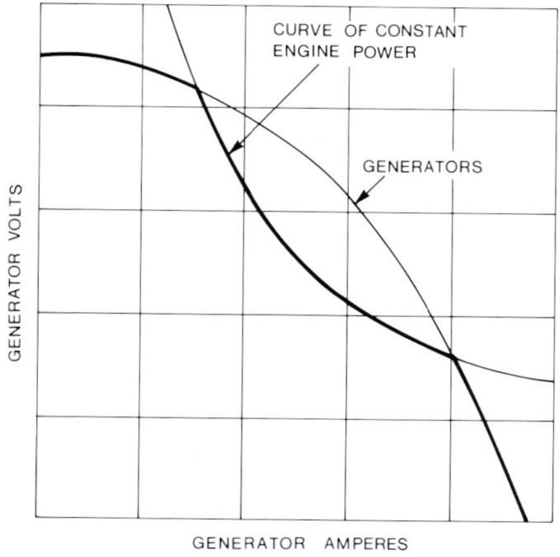

mechanically in most BR locomotives, but electronic control has been adopted in the most recent designs.

First, the diesel engine speed is controlled by the governor. This is based on rotating fly-weights and a spring. If the engine is running at the correct speed for the controller position, the centrifugal force of the fly-weights is balanced by the spring. If, however, the load on the engine is increased, the speed falls, the centrifugal force generated by the weights is reduced and they move inwards under the pressure of the spring. This movement is transmitted to a valve in the governor. As the valve opens it allows high pressure oil to flow to a piston which is connected to the fuel racks. The movement of the piston opens the fuel racks and the engine generates more power. When the output just exceeds the power demanded, the engine will speed up and when the correct speed is reached, the fly-wheel weights return to the position where the centrifugal force is balanced by the spring. In this position, the valve in the governor closes, shutting off the oil supply to the piston operating the fuel racks. In this over-simplified description the engine would, of course, hunt over and under the correct speed and in practice this is avoided by a system of restrictors in the oil system, compensating devices and feed-back.

A similar process is used to match the engine and generator characteristics. A further series of hydraulic valves and pistons in the governor regulates the flow of oil through an hydraulic vane motor which rotates a rheostat controlling the generator field excitation. Referring back to the previous example (Fig 8) and assuming that the engine was on part of the power curve below the generator characteristic, then even with the fuel racks fully open, the engine would not be able to generate sufficient power to match demand at the set speed. When maximum power is reached the engine is still underspeed and this causes the second hydraulic system in the governor to feed high pressure oil to the vane motor. This rotates the rheostat, which reduces the excitation of the field and unloads the generator until it matches the output of the diesel engine. Similarly, if the generator load is less than the engine power output selected by the driver, the engine will attempt to over-speed even when the fuel racks are at the minimum fuel position at that control setting. When this state is reached, the valve in the governor feeds high pressure oil into the other side of the vane motor which rotates the rheostat, increasing the excitation of the main generator field until demand equals supply again. In effect, the generator curve is made to fit the engine power curve between the two cross-over points.

The hydraulic control of both fuel racks and generator field excitation has practical advantages. An alternative system is to have electrical contacts which are closed by an overspeeding or underspeeding engine and cause an electric motor to rotate the rheostat in the appropriate direction.

With the advent of electronic control and solid state power devices it has been possible to eliminate the rheostat and instead control the alternator exciter field current by an electronic load regulator. In such designs — for example the Class 56 diesel locomotive — the displacement within the governor caused by over- or under-speeding is transformed into an electrical signal proportional to the movement from the neutral position and this signal is processed by the load controller to increase or decrease the field and return the transducer signal to neutral.

This description has been based on a fixed setting of the driver's controller. In practice there are several distinct steps or notches — five in the case of the HST — or power may be infinitely variable. Each notch corresponds to a different engine speed, the speed being varied by compressing the spring in the governor. In the Class 56 locomotive the spring is compressed pneumatically and the air pressure is varied continuously by the controller. As the compression in the spring is increased so the governor flyweights have to revolve faster to overcome the spring pressure and hence the governed engine speed increases, increasing the power output for any given fuel rack position. The functions of the driver's controller, governor and load regulator are shown schematically in Fig 9.

Fig 9 Elements of a diesel-electric locomotive control system

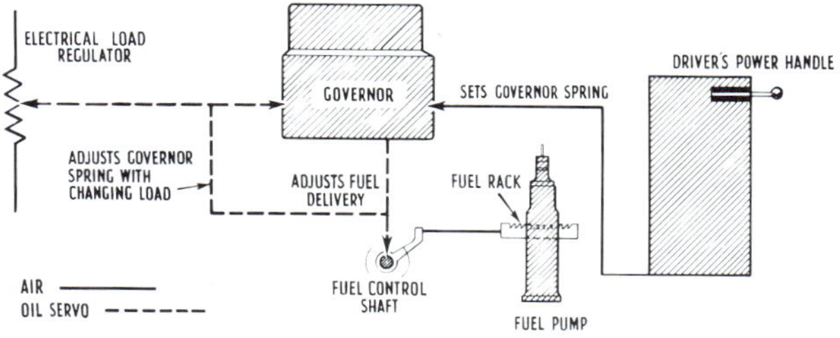

The change from dc to ac/dc transmission, coupled with solid state control equipment has greatly improved reliability of electrical equipment and reduced maintenance. However, it has complicated one aspect of diesel traction practice and that is engine starting. With dc generators, the engine can be started by running the generator as a motor off the locomotive's batteries. This is not possible with the alternator, and starter motors have had to be fitted to the latest stock. These operate through a geared pinion engaged with teeth on the engine flywheel.

Mechanical Transmission

British Rail diesel multiple-units have two types of mechanical transmission. One form, known as mechanical standard, is simply a rail version of the fluid flywheel and four-speed epicyclic gearbox drive train used in buses. The fluid flywheel is an outer housing which is connected to the engine and which contains a circular driven member which is connected to the gearbox. The outer housing is filled with oil. As the engine speeds up, the oil accelerates with the outer housing and impinges on cups in the driven member. This rotates the driven member which also accelerates until it is running at nearly the same speed as the engine. The gearbox is of the epicyclic type using permanently meshed sun and planet gearing. The overall gear ratio is changed by applying brakes to the internally-toothed annuli of the sun and planet gearing. Using three gears, braked in different combinations, four overall gear ratios are obtained. Each gear has to be selected by the driver and the movement of the gear handle changes gear electro-pneumatically.

The second type of transmission is the Rolls-Royce torque converter. This form of hydraulic transmission has an impeller driven by the engine. The impeller circulates oil through a series of turbine blades. There are three sets of blades on the output turbine disc, with stationary, or stator, blades after the first and second rings of turbine blades. Unlike the fluid flywheel, the impeller/turbine system provides torque multiplication. Thus at low road speed the engine output is converted into high torque at low revolutions per minute. As the train accelerates the output torque from the converter decreases as the rotational speed of the turbine rises. When the turbine speed equals the impeller speed, the impeller is disengaged from the engine by an oil-operated clutch and a second clutch engaged which gives direct drive.

5 Generators and Motors

In section 4 it was shown how the diesel engine converts the energy in its fuel into mechanical energy at the crankshaft, and it was noted that the generator driven by the engine may be an alternator or a direct current machine. Both generate current by the same basic method. When an electrical conductor cuts the lines of force of a magnetic field, an electromotive force is developed in it and will cause current to flow round any circuit connected to the conductor. In the direct current generator the electromagnets that produce the field are stationary, and the conductors are in the form of approximately U-shaped loops lying in slots around the periphery of a drum, or armature, driven by the engine. The two ends of each loop are connected to the segments of a rotating switch, or commutator. Carbon brushes held by spring pressure against the segments collect the current so that it can be fed to the traction motors. Were it not for the commutator the current in each coil would change direction once per revolution. The commutator is a mechanical rectifier causing the current in the external circuit to flow in one direction only.

In the type of alternator used in diesel-electric locomotives, however, the electromagnets revolve and the coils in which the currents are generated are stationary. The current is collected through static connections and no sliding contact such as that between commutator and brushes in a dc generator is required, the alternating current output being rectified externally by semiconductor rectifiers.

In both types of machine the electromagnets have to be excited by direct current. Excitation for a dc traction generator comes from an auxiliary machine coupled to the main one, involving a second commutator and set of brushes. Excitation for the revolving electromagnets of an alternator comes from an armature on the same shaft, the output from which is converted to dc by rectifiers mounted on the shaft and revolving with it. Thus no commutators or brushes are required either in the power or the excitation circuits and the machine is called a 'brushless alternator' as has been mentioned in Section 4.

The principle of the electric traction motor is the converse of that of the generator; the diagram of the basic electrical machine, Fig 10 applies to both. Only one coil of the armature winding is shown and the magnet is represented as a permanent magnet for simplicity. If the machine is supplied with current it will run as a motor. With the directions of magnetic field (N to S) and current round the loop shown, the right hand side of the loop experiences a downward-acting force, and the left-hand side an upward force, causing clockwise rotation. When the loop is vertical the coil is momentarily short-circuited by the brushes spanning the gaps between the commutator segments. As rotation continues, the descending coil side begins to rise and is now connected by the commutator to the negative brush so that it is subject to an upward force, while the other side connected to the positive brush, is now forced downwards. Rotation therefore continues. When the directions of field and current in a motor are known, the direction of rotation can be found by the 'Left Hand Rule' (see any electrical text book).

In a practical motor there would be two or three pairs of main poles and a large number of armature coils and commutator segments. The magnets would be electromagnets and in order to provide excitation the current leaving the negative brush would flow through field windings on the poles on its way back to the negative pole of the supply. There would also be smaller poles, called 'interpoles', between the pairs of main poles. When armature and

Fig 10
Electric motor and generator fundamentals

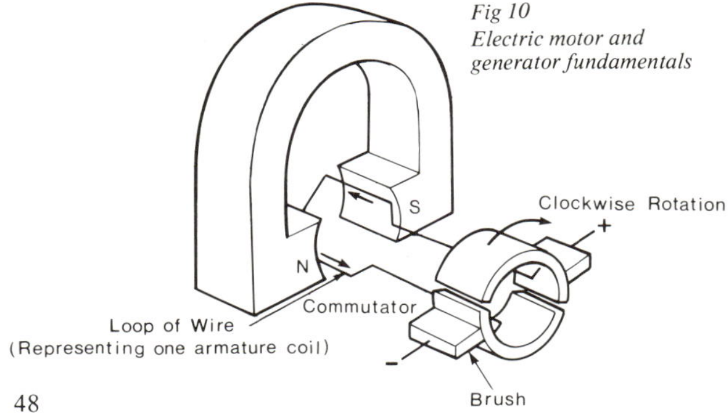

Above: Rotor shaft of a Class 56 freight locomotive generator, showing from left to right the cooling fan, rotating field systems of the main and auxiliary generators, the two exciter rotors, and on extreme right the rotating diode assembly which rectifies the exciter outputs; the whole group constitutes the essentials of a 'brushless alternator'. Brush Electrical Machines

field windings are connected in sequence in the manner described the motor is called a 'series motor', and because of the high torque, or turning effort, developed at low speed this type has been almost universal in traction for many years. With the development of thyristor control, however, it is often the practice to excite the field windings separately, but the excitation is variable in such a way that the motor still has series characteristics at starting.

Commutation — the sudden reversal of current in a coil — is a drastic process and can produce violent sparking at the brushes if it does not take place in the correct conditions. Referring again to the diagram, when the coil is passing through the vertical it is short-circuited by the brushes spanning the gaps between the commutator segments, and it is in a 'neutral' position because the sides are moving parallel to the lines of force instead of cutting through them. The interpoles are positioned so that at this moment they induce in the coil an emf acting in the direction in which the current will flow when the brushes again contact the individual segments.

The current flowing in the armature coil sets up a magnetic field around it which reacts with the main field and, in the absence of

interpoles, would tend to shift the neural point in one direction or the other. If the brushes were left in the theoretical neutral position, the coil when short-circuited would still be in the influence of the main field, which would induce in it an emf in the *opposite* direction to that in which the current next has to flow. At one time the difficulty was overcome by shifting the brushes, but it was necessary to change their setting when the motor had to run in the opposite direction. This was no great problem for some industrial motors which nearly always ran the same way, but obviously impracticable for a traction motor. The introduction of interpoles was therefore a vital step in the development of the modern traction machine.

In some circumstances field-weakening can displace the neutral position in spite of the interpoles; to overcome this effect an additional winding called a 'compensating winding' may be fitted into slots in the pole faces.

Left: Frame of a traction motor for a Class 87 ac electric locomotive, showing main pole faces, an interpole, and the compensating winding to improve commutation at low field strengths. GEC Traction Ltd

Above: A traction motor and drive system of a Class 82 ac electric locomotive. Note the pinion on the motor shaft, the gearwheel on the axle, and, outside the driving wheel, the rubber-bushed linkage through which the torque is transmitted from axle to wheel. GEC Traction Ltd

To reverse a series motor the direction of current through the field windings is changed, without changing the direction of flow through the armature coils. If both were changed together the motor would simply continue running in the same direction.

If instead of being supplied with current the armature of the machine shown in the diagram were rotated mechanically in the same direction, the effect of the conductors cutting the lines of force would be to set up emfs in them such that current would flow round the loop in the *opposite* direction to the arrows. The motor has become a generator, just as happens in rheostatic braking when the armatures are disconnected from the supply but field excitation continues. Note that through the commutator segments the *descending* side of the coil is always connected to the same brush, and the same applies to the ascending side. The current at the terminals is therefore uni-directional. If an ac output were required the commutator would be replaced by two sliprings, one connected to each end of the coil, with current collected through brushes as before, but as has been seen already, in a practical traction alternator current is collected from a stationary winding.

6 Diesel Locomotives and dmus

by B. Cooper and C. J. Leigh

Some of the experiments with diesel locomotives and railcars during the Grouping years were short-lived but two companies embarked on policies which had a lasting influence. Experiments with diesel shunting power undertaken in 1933 by the LMSR paved the way for the standard 350hp diesel-electric shunter, and in the following year the Great Western began operating a streamlined diesel-mechanical railcar on local services from Southall. At the company's annual general meeting in February 1935 the GWR Chairman said that cars of this type would be used 'on local services where the traffic is not of sufficient volume to justify running an ordinary train or even a steam railcar', and he went on to announce that more powerful vehicles were operating as a three-car train with buffet service between Birmingham and Cardiff.

Diesel locomotives

After World War II the LMSR and the Southern Railway both announced plans for main line diesel traction. The LMS locomotives were the 1,600hp diesel-electrics Nos 10000 and 10001, and a mixed traffic unit, No 10800. No 10000 just managed to appear in LMS days, being driven out of the diesel shop at Derby on 8 December 1947 by H. G. Ivatt, Acting Chief Mechanical Engineer of the LMSR. The first of three Southern locomotives was not completed until 1951.

At first BR policy was to meet immediate motive power requirements by building standard classes of new steam locomotives but in 1954 the first multiple-unit diesel trains were introduced, carrying forward the practice initiated by the GWR 20 years earlier except that the Great Western had operated local services with single vehicles. There was much optimism that the dmus would revive flagging local traffic and allow continued economic operation of lines that were lightly used. Large orders were placed for diesel shunters but there was no further move in main line dieselisation until the Modernisation Plan of 1955 announced the policy of replacing steam completely with diesel or electric traction. Under the Plan 174 diesel locomotives were ordered with outputs ranging from 800 to 2,300hp.

Germany was making successful use of main line diesel locomotives with hydraulic transmission, a system which at that time showed a more favourable ratio of power to weight than was being achieved with electric transmission. Hydraulic transmission was adopted on the Western Region, which received its first A1A-A1A 'Warships' in 1958. They were followed by three B-B classes and finally the 2,700hp C-C 'Westerns', the last of which was withdrawn in 1977. Hydraulic transmission did not remain unchallenged in the Region throughout that period. Some 1,750hp diesel-electrics (now Class 37) were ordered in 1962 and the performance of the two systems was compared in similar conditions. A report published in 1965 showed that differences in power/weight ratio were being narrowed, and in a comparison between a 'Hymek' 1,700hp diesel-hydraulic and a Class 37 the diesel-electric had the advantage in availability, first cost, and casualties. Electric transmission was also favoured by the trend towards higher powers because a single hydraulic transmission could not handle more than about 2,000hp. The 'Warships' (2,000 and 2,200hp) and the 'Westerns' all had two engines and two transmissions. Electric transmission has now been standardised for diesel locomotives and is to be adopted in future diesel multiple-unit construction.

Below: Two Class 20 locomotives, Nos 20.050 and 20.026, head a northbound coke train through the cutting north of Masboro, near Rotherham. L. A. Nixon

Of the current diesel classes on BR, Class 20 is the only fully operational survivor of the 800-1,000hp range originally classified as 'Type 1'. It was also the first to be delivered under the Plan, appearing in May 1957. The single cab and the 'bonnet' enclosing the engine-generator set were characteristic of this power range when introduced, although the later 'Claytons' had a central cab and two bonnets, with an engine-generator set under each. Class 20 was designed and built by The English Electric Co Ltd, which was the only British company able to supply a complete diesel-electric locomotive from within its own organisation, the mechanical parts being built at the company's Vulcan Foundry. This 1,000hp Bo-Bo design was intended mainly for freight and freight transfer work, having no train heating boiler, although it was said from the first that they would be used on certain passenger duties in the summer months. They can still be seen so employed on excursions and extras.

October 1957 saw the first Type 2 — the present Class 31. The first of the series had Mirrlees engines rated at 1,250hp. Construction of bogies and underframes was shared by Beyer, Peacock and W. G. Bagnall, but the main contractor was the Brush Electrical Engineering Co Ltd and the locomotives were erected in that company's works at Loughborough. The name 'Brush Type 2' has stuck. These are the only survivors on BR of the A1A-A1A wheel arrangement. The weight of 104 tons is carried on two three-axle bogies in which only the outer axles are motored and the central carrying axle has wheels of smaller diameter than the drivers (3ft 3.5in against 3ft 7in). In the first of the series the power handle moved in the vertical plane (like the HST power controller today) instead of horizontally, and it had a 'one-knob' control. When the handle was in the 'off' position the knob was twisted to select 'engine start', 'engine only', 'forward', 'neutral', or 'reverse'. When a function had been selected, the handle could be moved forward to increase power in steps.

In the course of their careers the 31s were uprated and some were equipped with 1,600hp engines. All are now powered by English Electric engines of 1,470hp.

Engine 'families' form a convenient way of grouping the BR diesel fleet. One of them goes back well before the Plan and its latest descendants are at work in Class 56 today. The English Electric SVT series made its debut on BR in the 16-cylinder 1,600hp engine

Above: Class 31 No 31.401 passes Twerton, approaching Bath, with the 11.15 Bristol-Portsmouth. John Chalcraft

of Nos 10000/01. By the time the first of the Southern main line diesels appeared in 1951 basically the same engine was giving 1,750hp, and the first 2,000hp version took to the rails in the third of the Southern locomotives in 1954. In April 1958 English Electric delivered the first of the present Class 40s, again with the 2,000hp engine. Another link with the Southern diesels is the plate frame bogie with three driving axles and a pony truck within the main bogie frame, giving the 1Co-Co1 wheel arrangement. The locomotive body is supported directly on the bogie by segmental bearings which allow pivoting. Eight axles carry the weight of 133 tons, and the overall length is an impressive 69ft 6in. The styling of the locomotive, with a 'nose' at each end, was soon to become familiar. Each nose compartment houses a traction motor blower for the adjacent bogie and an exhauster or compressor. At one time the nose was commended because it prevented a direct view of the track immediately below the driver, guiding his line of sight forward and so avoiding the distracting effect of what was called 'sleeper flicker'. Experience has shown, however, that judicious cab design can avoid the problem. In their early years the 40s were often criticised for their low power in comparison with what a contemporary steam Pacific locomotive could produce, but at least 2,000hp were always on tap, ready to come rumbling forth at a touch on a handle, which was not always noticeably the case with the steam locomotives of the day. Cylinders of the Class 40 engine are of the same dimensions as those of the eight-cylinder

Above: Class 37 (left) No 37.080 passes No 47.378 at Pengam with a freight from Severn Tunnel Junction to Tidal Sidings. M. Rhode

engine in Class 20, and many components of the two engines are common to both.

By 1961 charge-air cooling enabled a 12-cylinder version of the SVT series to give 1,750hp at 850rev/min. This engine powers the English Electric Type 3 locomotive (Class 37). Output per cylinder is 146bhp, compared with 125bhp in the 16-cylinder engine in Class 40. Weighing 103 tons, Class 37 has a power/weight ratio of 16.99hp ton as against 15.03hp/ton for the earlier locomotives. The distinctive 'nose' of the Class 40s is retained, again housing a blower and a compressor or exhauster, although in other classes introduced at the same period the 'nose' was becoming snub by comparison. In Class 37 the Co-Co wheel arrangement resulted in a shorter and more compact looking locomotive, 61ft 6in in overall length. In previous English Electric designs the load regulator had been driven by an electric pilot motor but here the change was made to oil servo drive.

Class 37 appeared in a period of transition when BR was looking for higher powers than had been proposed in the original Plan. It is convenient at this point, therefore, to look back at the parallel development of another 'family' of engines — the Sulzer LDA and LVA series.

The Sulzer LDA series evolved over the years from its introduction in 1935 on the Continent, and in its final form comprised a steel underbed and crankcase and cast steel cross members, all welded up as one unit, surmounted by a mild steel welded cylinder block with cast iron wet liners. A special form of main bearing construction, with the bearing caps inserted between shoulders in the cast steel cross members, added stiffness and in combination with the welded construction was claimed to provide a degree of rigidity specially appropriate for rail traction.

Large numbers of general-purpose Bo-Bo locomotives were built in the Type 2 category (1,000-1,500hp), the first, in 1958, being Class 24, nominally withdrawn in 1977 but exhibiting noteworthy powers of survival. This was a BR design with the Sulzer 6-cylinder in-line 6LDA-28 engine of 1,160hp at 750rev/min and BTH electrical equipment. Construction was shared by BR and Beyer-Peacock. Also in 1958 the first Class 26s were delivered by the Birmingham Railway Carriage & Wagon Co Ltd. They, too, have the 6LDA-28 engine but Crompton Parkinson electrics, a feature of which is the recessing of the auxiliary generator armature into the commutator hub of the main generator, both machines being contained within one frame.

At this period the first stage of electrification of the Southern Region's Kent Coast lines was nearing completion. Most passenger

Below: Class 40 No 40.057 passes Pilmoor with the 15.10 Liverpool Lime Street-Newcastle express. John E. Oxley

services were to be worked by emus, but for certain duties and for freight, locomotives were necessary. They comprised the Class 71 electrics, now withdrawn, and the Class 33 diesel-electrics.

Powered by an eight-cylinder version of the LDA engine — 8LDA 28 — the Class 33s when introduced in 1960 came into the Type 3 classification with a rating of 1,550hp. This was another BRCW/Crompton product, but it was more than simply a more powerful Class 26 in that the engine-generator set included a generator for electric train heating. Since that time large numbers of other diesel locomotives originally fitted with train heating boilers have been modified to provide electric train heating. The Class 33s are Southern-based but excursion workings often take them far afield. When the Bournemouth line was electrified in 1967, 19 locomotives were equipped for push-pull working of emu trailer coaches between Bournemouth and Weymouth in order to provide

Left: Class 25 No 25.137 heads a loaded ore train from the ICI Quarries, Tunstead, through Chinley towards Manchester. L. A. Nixon

Above: Class 27 No 27.210 in harness with No 27.201 at the rear mounts the 1 in 42 incline out of Glasgow Queen Street with a push-pull train to Edinburgh. G. A. Watt

a through Waterloo-Weymouth service. The locomotives so modified form Class 33/1; their remote control equipment also enables them to work in multiple with emus or electro-diesels. Another variant is Class 33/2, built to the loading gauge of the Tonbridge-Hastings line. These have a slow-speed control for working merry-go-round (mgr) trains, enabling the driver to select a speed in the 0-3mile/h range, which is held automatically while the train passes through the loading or unloading points at collieries and power stations.

From 1961 new BR/Beyer, Peacock Bo-Bos were powered by a larger LDA engine than the original series, the 6LDA-28B of 1,250hp, and locomotives with this installation formed Class 25. The original 25/0 batch has AEI electrical equipment, while the 25/1, 25/2 and 25/3 versions have GEC equipment with detail differences between them. The same engine went into Class 27, also introduced in 1961, another BRCW product but this time with GEC equipment. Classes 27/1 and 27/2 were fitted for push-pull operation of fast trains on the Edinburgh-Glasgow service, with one locomotive at each end of the train. The 27/2 version has electric train heating as well. In 1979 push-pull trains with a single modified Class 47 locomotive and a driving trailer began to replace the dual-27 sets.

On the eve of the 1960s interest was beginning to centre on horsepowers in the range between 2,000 and 3,000. BR's own Type 4 design, the 2,300hp 'Peak' class, was unveiled in 1959 and introduced another engine in the Sulzer LDA series. This was the 12-cylinder 12LDA-28, which has two banks of vertical cylinders and two crankshafts geared to a common output shaft. Mechanically the design was again a 1Co-Co1 with the 'traditional' plate frame bogies of the first Southern diesels and the Class 40s. Contemporary eyebrows were raised at the weight of 138 tons. Only 10 'Peaks' (Class 44) were built but they were quickly followed by the mechanically similar and still numerous locomotives of Classes 45 and 46 in which an intercooled version of the 12LDA-28 engines — the 12LDA-28B — raised the rating to 2,500hp.

The range between 2,500 and 3,000hp continued to interest British Railways. In May 1962 a consortium consisting of AEI, BRCW, and Sulzer handed over to BR a 2,750hp prototype Co-Co locomotive, *Lion*, with a larger version of the 12LDA-28B engine. The design was not perpetuated but the engine was adopted for

Below: Class 47 No 47.429 with Mk III coaches forms a York-Liverpool Lime Street express leaving Huddersfield. A. R. Kaye

BR's eventual choice of a locomotive in this category. This was the 2,750hp Brush Type 4 (Class 47), the first of which was delivered later in the same year. In recent years the 12LDA-28C engines in the 47s have been reset to give 2,580hp at 750rev/min. The design has a full-length body and swing-bolster six-wheel bogies with all axles motored; weight is 117 tons. The first 20 locomotives of the class had train heating generators. Many more are now equipped for electric train heating but with an alternator which provides both auxiliary supplies at 110V and a train heating output at 850V.

In all these locomotives the gearing between the two crankshafts and the output shaft gives a generator speed of 1,080rev/min for an engine speed of 750rev/min, enabling the electrical machines to be smaller and lighter than if they were driven direct.

As well as the Type 4 design which was accepted by BR, Brush had built a prototype 2,800hp diesel-electric, *Falcon*, with two high-speed (1,500rev/min) engines similar to those in the 'Western' class diesel-hydraulics which appeared in the same year, 1962. Each engine drove a generator supplying power to the motors of one bogie. The aim of showing that a diesel-electric locomotive could rival the power/weight ratio of a diesel-hydraulic, was achieved. *Falcon* weighed 115 tons (24.3hp/ton) as compared with the 'Western' weight of 105 tons for 2,700hp (25.7hp/ton). High-speed engines demanded more maintenance, however, and larger stocks of spares had to be carried for maintaining twin-engined locomotives. *Falcon* remained unique. It worked on the Western Region, its natural home in view of its engines, in its later years and was withdrawn in the early 1970s.

English Electric also constructed a prototype in the same power bracket. Its 'DP2' locomotive foreshadowed the Co-Co Class 50 of 1967, having an intercooled 16SVT engine giving 2,700hp at 850rev/min. Class 50 introduced more advanced equipment than had been the practice before — some thought it too advanced. Two of the new features were rheostatic braking and electronic control of tractive effort at a pre-set level during acceleration, with detection and correction of wheelslip claimed to operate within half a revolution of the wheels.

Class 50 locomotives operating in pairs were given the task of working accelerated schedules between Crewe and Glasgow after the southern portion of the West Coast main line was fully electrified. When electrification was extended from Weaver Junction

Above: Class 50 No 50.040 is at Dainton with the 14.23 Paddington-Plymouth express. D. Kimber

to Glasgow in 1974 the class was transferred to the Western Region, but its duties here diminished as more HSTs came into service. Some 50s were then earmarked for the Waterloo-Exeter service and also for the Northeast-Southwest route via Birmingham in advance of HST services.

Up to and including Class 50 all BR diesel-electric locomotives had direct current generators. In 1968 Hawker Siddeley (with which Brush was by then merged) completed a 4,000hp prototype locomotive as a private venture. The engine was a Sulzer 16-cylinder vee type of the LVA series and it drove a three-phase traction generator. A rectifier of 84 silicon diodes converted the output into dc for the six traction motors. In general the electrical equipment was similar to that supplied by Brush for the present Class 56 freight locomotives, although in Class 56 10 years of development of semiconductor power rectifiers has enabled the number of diodes to be halved.

Kestrel ran dynamometer trials on BR, but as built its axle-load of nearly 24 tons was considered too high for it to run at its designed maximum speed of 125mile/h. Class 47 bogies were substituted and for a time the locomotive worked passenger trains between London and Newcastle. It was later transferred to coal trains between Tinsley and March, but after a request was received from the USSR railways to exhibit *Kestrel* at an international

Fig 11 Equipment layout of a Class 56 freight locomotive

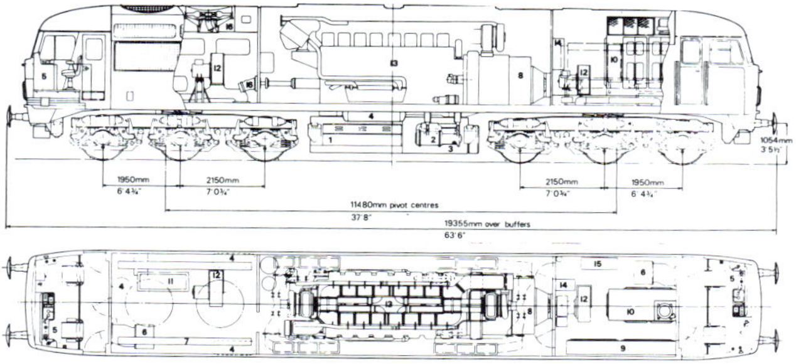

exhibition near Moscow, negotiations were begun for its purchase. Terms were agreed and *Kestrel* was formally handed over to the Soviet Railways at Scherbinka on 16 July 1971.

Class 56 (Fig 11) does not quite match the 4,000hp of *Kestrel* but its GEC Diesels engine is set to give 3,250hp. It is a direct descendant of the English Electric 16SVT series and typifies the progress achieved in diesel engine design for traction since Nos 10000/01. The class was designed with the haulage of merry-go-round trains between collieries and power stations specifically in mind. This duty involves hauling a payload of about 1,000 tons and

Below: Class 55 ('Deltic') No 55.003, Meld, *stands at the head of the 'Hull Executive' at Kings Cross.* Roger Goode

Above: Class 56 No 56.037 leaves Drakelow power station (near Burton-on-Trent) with a train of empties. C. J. Tuffs

Above right: Class 33/1 No 33.119 takes the Weymouth portion of the 13.30 from Waterloo out of Dorchester South. G. F. Gillham

Right: Heavy trains for the steel industry are worked by three Class 37s equipped for working in multiple. Nos 37.304, 143 and 307 wind a long line of empties out of Llanwern steel works, contrasting with the single brakevan load of No 37.142 on the left. L. Bertram

maintaining a constant low speed during loading and unloading operations in spite of the continuously varying load. The driver of a Class 56 sets a low-speed control at one of three positions and after he has applied power the selected speed is maintained by the electronic control system without further action on his part. In earlier versions of this control, as fitted in Classes 47, 33 and 20, small 'trimming' adjustments have to be made while a locomotive is working in a low-speed mode. Design work on a more powerful diesel-electric freight locomotive, Class 58, in the 3,500-4,000hp range, was in progress in 1980.

So far we have dealt with the main stream of diesel development on BR. A noteworthy exception is Class 55, equally well known as the 'Deltics' from the name of the prototype, now in the Science

Museum. The original 'Deltic' was built by English Electric to gain experience in railway traction with the Napier opposed-piston two-stroke engine, which had been designed for Admiralty requirements. Weighing only 106 tons for 3,300hp (31.1hp/ton), the prototype was a notable improvement on its diesel-electric contemporaries; between 1955 and withdrawal in 1961 it ran 400,000 miles in main line service but always remained the property of the builder.

High-speed engines and twin-engined locomotives such as the 'Deltic' were not much favoured by BR at the time, but the General Manager of the Eastern Region saw in the design the answer to his own requirements on the East Coast main line. He obtained approval for an order for 22 production locomotives, which were

delivered between March 1961 and March 1962. They were run in on a variety of light and heavy revenue duties in readiness for the introduction of a full timetable based on 'Deltic' haulage in June 1962. The Class 55 'Deltics' weigh only 99 tons (33.3hp ton). Certain changes were made from the prototype, notably in the bogies, which are interchangeable with those of Class 37, and in the introduction of step-down gearing between the engines and the generators, giving an armature speed of 1,125rev/min at the engine speed of 1,500rev/min. Some constructional changes altered the

Left: Motor bogie of a Class 40 locomotive showing the segmental bearings on which the body pivots and side bearers of the leading pony truck at the far end. Similar bogies are used in Classes 45 and 46. Ian Allan Library

Above: Class 45 No 45.104 on an up express recovers from a pw check north of Luton. Kevin Lane

appearance slightly compared with the prototype and increased the overall length from 64ft to 69ft 6in. Like the Western Region with its diesel-hydraulics, the East Coast main line possessed in the 'Deltics' a locomotive fleet as characteristic as once the Gresley Pacifics had been, and that at a period when the express train was beginning to lose individuality by the wide dispersal of other classes of mainline diesel-electrics. From 1978 'Deltic' duties began to be taken over by IC125 sets on the ECML but it is expected that there will be work for them at least until 1982 even if not always on their traditional ground. In the 1979 timetable a 'Deltic' had BR's fastest-ever locomotive-hauled timing on the 17.05 'Hull Executive' from Kings Cross, being booked to cover the 138½ miles to passing Retford in 91 min at an average speed of 91.32mile/h.

The BR diesel with the longest pedigree is the standard 350hp de shunter. Many detail changes of equipment have taken place since the 1930s but the shunter is still an 0-6-0 with two traction motors, one driving each outer axle through double-reduction gearing. Class 08 is geared for a top speed of 20mile/h but Class 09 has a different ratio to give a top speed of 27mile/h. The intermediate gear shafts are removable so that the axles can be disconnected from the traction motors when a locomotive has to be towed. Provision is made for connecting the motors in series (normal) or parallel according to the duties the locomotive has to perform but this change can only be made 'off load' with the engine shut down. Automatic load control is not provided, efficient use of engine power over the small speed range involved being inherent in the design of the electrical machines. The driver's controller is mechanically coupled to the engine governor. Early notches increase the generator excitation in steps by cutting out resistance, with the engine running at constant speed. Further movement of the controller provides continuous control of engine speed up to maximum.

Diesel Multiple-Units

Both the London Midland and Scottish Railway and the Great Western experimented with the use of diesel-mechanical railcars during the 1930s. Such was the success of the GWR vehicles that many of them survived into the early 1960s, to be replaced by the influx of new BR units.

Much has been written about the politics of BRs rush into dieselisation and the choice of the diesel-mechanical unit for the bulk of secondary, branch and suburban services in many areas. To be fair, the choice was limited, and faced with the need to replace large amounts of ancient life-expired stock and locomotives with something more efficient and economical, the dmu was a logical choice.

The first units to enter BR service arrived on the scene in 1954, a year before the Modernisation Plan which heralded the purchase of large numbers from various different manufacturers. These pioneer units were the original Derby lightweight' twin units, consisting of a motor coach and driving trailer car. The basic layout was standard for most subsequent units, employing a motor coach with underfloor-mounted engines and a standardised mechanical

Above: The 15.20 St Pancras-Bedford is formed by a 'Derby' four-car suburban dmu, seen approaching Harlington. Les Bertram

transmission. The body design had large windows with top vents, bus-type seats and large cab windows, through which front seat passengers were treated to the novelty of the view ahead. The Derby lightweight units went into service initially in the West Riding, the Lake District and North Wales, but the lightweight aluminium body was not perpetuated and the units had a fairly short life. None is now in passenger service but one twin unit was converted to form the Ultrasonic Rail test train, while one of the two single-unit railcars built to the same basic design is used by the Railway Technical Centre at Derby under the name Test Coach *Iris*.

During the late 1950s the first deliveries of most of the major types were made, and many of these are still in regular daily use. For convenience of description they can be divided into three main groups, suburban, cross-country and inter-city units as they were originally known, or high, medium and low-density in current parlance. The newer description is an indication of seating capacity. In addition to these groups there were some special types such as the diesel Pullman units and the Southern Region's diesel-electric units.

Suburban Types

These constitute by far the largest proportion of the dmu fleet and consist of a variety of types from several manufacturers. Among the earliest examples were those built by Metropolitan Cammell, having a distinctive body shape with small windows with top vents and an

Above: Class 47 No 47.429 lifts the 13.12 Sheffield-Edinburgh up the bank near Burnmouth. L. A. Nixon

Above right: Class 203 diesel-electric buffet unit No 1035 at Tonbridge on a Charing Cross-Hastings service. John Scrace

angular cab end. They were formed into two, three, or four car sets, gangwayed within the set, and worked initially on all regions except the WR and SR. Although most examples contained seating in the medium-high density category the larger units with toilets and some with miniature buffets were used on a variety of longer distance services.

Some early Metro-Cammell sets with non-standard equipment have been withdrawn, but the majority are still in service and have been included in the refurbishing scheme to update them for use until about 1990. The refurbishing includes improvements to heating, lighting and insulation as well as internal redecoration. Such units were distinguished by a revised livery of white body with a blue band at waist level but have now reverted to normal blue and grey.

Most other suburban types possess a certain family likeness in having a standard body style employing a plain window with no top vent, and doors to each seating bay. In this category come the main series of Derby-built units as well as examples built for the Western

Region by Pressed Steel and Birmingham RC&W. These, with the exception of LMR London area units, were originally three-car sets having a trailer composite with toilet, marshalled between a motor second and a motor brake second. The body design of the various builds was virtually identical with only a little variation in the treatment of the standard cab end. These were provided with a four-character headcode panel at roof height (Pressed Steel and Birmingham sets) or in the case of Derby units a variety of headlight or headlight plus two-character headcode configurations.

The Western Region also acquired some 36 single unit railcars as direct descendants of their original streamlined cars, for branch services. The first twenty, supplied by Gloucester RC&W were similar to the Derby suburban units in having the same body style with two-character headcode display. The units contained a guard's/luggage compartment, seating for 65 second class passengers and a driving cab at each end. The exhaust pipes which were carried on the 'inner' end of most dmus had on the single units to be carried up one cab end. The Gloucester units were put to work in 1958 on London area branch services, from which they were ousted in 1960 by the 16 Pressed Steel single units. These were identical in most major respects, save for the provision of the four-character headcode display.

The Gloucester units were transferred away to the Midlands and the south-west and were soon devastated by branch service closures. Only half now remain in passenger service, on the Scottish and London Midland Regions. Most of the others survive in departmental service as route learning cars. The Pressed Steel single units mostly survive in service on some branch and secondary routes, but also see considerable service as stand-ins for vehicles missing from three-car units.

The Western and London Midland Regions both operate a few single unit parcels vans constructed by Gloucester RC&W. Again these are descendants of earlier GWR vehicles. There are nine vehicles (Class 128), six of which are fitted with end gangways, and they have a large parcels stowage area with six sets of wide sliding doors for access. Each car has a pair of 230bhp Leyland Albion engines, making them more powerful than most passenger dmus cars and enabling a tail-load of vans to be hauled. To increase the haulage capacity the cars sometimes operate with downgraded passenger power cars which have had their seating removed.

The LMR uses some Derby-built four-car units on suburban services out of St Pancras, and these are basically similar to the WR units but with an additional trailer vehicle and four-character headcode display. Unlike their WR sisters which have been equipped with gangways for 'Paytrain' operation, the LMR sets remain non-gangwayed.

Most suburban units which are expected to remain in service up to 1990 are included in the refurbishing programme. The LMR four-car sets are not included as they are to be displaced by electrification. Many sets equipped with headcode displays have had these removed or blanked off since the decision to abandon this form of train identification.

Cross-Country Types

Only two types of unit were actually designated as cross-country versions when they first appeared, those built by Gloucester RC&W, and a similar series built at Swindon. However this category also covers many of the Metro-Cammell sets and some of the older Birmingham RC&W sets with lower seating capacity. A few low-density Park Royal and Gloucester twin sets, both of which types are being phased out, can also be included here.

The Gloucester and Swindon three-car sets have seating in open saloons and the trailer car contains a miniature buffet in place of one seating bay. In practice, these buffets have seen little use. As built each seating bay was provided with a small table, but these

Above: A Class 119 Gloucester 'Cross-Country' dmu enters Newbury with a Bedwyn-Reading working. D. E. Canning

have now been removed. Both types have the same body configuration for the three cars, but while the Gloucester units have a standard 'Derby' cab end, the Swindon types have a distinctive more angular end with only two windows.

A switch round of stock during 1978 has resulted in most of the Gloucester built sets being allocated to the Western Region while many of the Swindon ones have gone to LMR.

The original Gloucester and Park Royal twin units are similar in general body style to the original Derby lightweight design and employed the same 56ft underframe. There are a few survivors in both these classes, but they are being withdrawn as they become surplus. The few twin units built by Wickham also had the short underframe and similar bodywork but possessed a highly individual interior treatment. One of these units has been extensively modified and is retained in immaculate order as the ER General Manager's saloon. It is the only survivor in the UK, several of its sisters having been shipped to Trinidad upon withdrawal.

Above: Class 123 'Inter-City' dmu passes Grindleford with the 11.45 Manchester Piccadilly-Sheffield. L. P. Gater

Inter-City Types

The first 'inter-city' dmus were the three or six-car sets built at Swindon for the Scottish Region and introduced just before the outwardly similar cross-country units. At this time the 'inter-city' title applied to the units had not been adopted as a general marketing title for main line passenger services.

The Scottish Region units introduced a number of unusual features for dmus including some side-corridor compartment vehicles and also intermediate motor seconds with end gangway and driving cab at one side. Each three-car set had one conventional motor second with full width driving cab and another of the intermediate type with gangway. Two sets could thus be coupled back to back to form a six-car set in which all passengers had access to the buffet trailer car which was included in one of the three-car sets.

These units were displaced from Glasgow-Edinburgh services by locomotive-hauled trains and vehicles were reformed into conventional three-car sets for sale abroad. A few surviving vehicles remain in service, including some of the intermediate motor seconds.

The Swindon-built six-car Trans-Pennine units built for the then North Eastern Region are readily distinguished by the glass fibre cab end with wrap-around windows similar to that used on the ScR electric units. The original formation of these strikingly individual units included a buffet car, but these have now been removed, reducing the units to five cars. The motor coaches of these units employed the more powerful 230bhp Leyland Albion engine.

One of the last dmu designs to enter traffic were the three-and four-car inter-city units built at Swindon for the Western Region. These also had the Leyland Albion engine, and the motor coaches had a gangwayed version of the glass fibre cab front — the only dmus so fitted. They worked various WR services including some cross-country Cardiff-Portsmouth runs from 1963 onwards but after a period in store, all were transferred to Hull in 1977. They have since been restored to traffic on the Trans-Pennine routes replacing the earlier Swindon units.

Other Types

No survey of the BR diesel unit fleet would be complete without mention of the celebrated 'Blue Pullmans'. These sets combined all the luxury and individuality of traditional Pullman travel in a diesel powered multiple unit. Two six-car units were supplied to the LMR, and three eight-car sets to the Western Region. The LMR sets were first class only while the extra vehicles in the WR sets enabled second class accommodation to be included. The sets had a 90mile/h top speed and in their eye-catching 'steel-blue' and white livery they were arguably the most impressive trains of the 1960s. By 1970 the LMR sets had been displaced by electrification and transferred to the WR where they found little use. All were repainted into uninspired grey livery in which they soon became dirty and unkempt. Riding of the sophisticated bogies and suspension deteriorated with age, and wholesale withdrawals of NBL/MAN-engined locomotives finally caught up with them. In their formation and high power-weight ratio they were perhaps the shape of things to come on the WR.

The Southern Region diesel units represent an entirely different concept from those on the other regions. Because the SR desired a high degree of standardisation with its electric stock it opted for heavyweight all-steel units with diesel-electric power plant. The need for a more substantial engine and a bulky generator meant that these components must be mounted above the floor, with consequent loss of passenger accommodation. The first SR two and three-car diesel units were outwardly similar to the 2HAP type electric units with the exception of the large engine compartment.

These were followed by two types of six-car sets built to the

Above: Class 205 dmu No 1128 at Bristol Temple Meads on a Portsmouth service. G. Scott-Lowe

narrow-bodied Hastings line profile, the main difference between the two types being in the length of underframe. These units are provided with a 500hp motor coach at either end, and although some units possess buffet cars, the sets are gangwayed only within each unit. The combination of the flat coach sides and the standard non-gangwayed 'Eastleigh' cab front has produced a unit of quite exceptionally ugly and antiquated appearance. However, the SR diesel-electric units do have a commendable record of reliability.

The most recent of the SR demus are 19 three-car units sets built for Oxted line services in 1962. Although they employ a traditional suburban type body, the design was modernised and a cab front with rounded corners is employed. The motor coach has a 600hp power unit mounted above the floor as in the earlier units. Six hybrid units were formed in 1964 using spare Hastings line power cars and trailers with a 2HAP type driving trailer car. Known as 'tadpoles' because of the curious effect created by coaches of different widths used in the sets, they provided Reading-Redhill-Tonbridge services but in 1979 were replaced by diesel-mechanical units based on the Western Region.

Most of the refurbished dmu types and many Swindon and Gloucester cross-country units which are currently being re-engined are likely to remain in service until 1990. In the meantime a standard diesel-electric unit is being developed as a replacement for these units which will by then have a service record longer than much of the equipment supplied under the 1955 Modernisation Plan.

7 Electric Traction and Motive Power

Throughout the first half of the 20th century railway electrification in Great Britain was mainly with direct current conductor rail systems at between 600 and 700V. Exceptions up to World War II were the 1,200V dc system between Manchester and Bury with a special protected conductor rail, and four electrifications with overhead contact wire, two dc and two ac. The dc overhead systems, both at 1,500V, were the Newport-Shildon freight electrification of the North Eastern Railway and the Manchester South Junction & Altrincham Joint line. Electric working on the Newport-Shildon line was abandoned in 1935.

The two ac systems were in the London suburban area of the London Brighton & South Coast Railway and on the Lancaster-Morecambe-Heysham lines of the Midland Railway. Both used a single-phase supply at 25Hz to avoid the problems of operating series traction motors at the industrial frequency of 50Hz. After the formation of the Southern Railway in 1923 the LBSCR electrification was converted to 660V dc with third rail to conform with other electrified lines in the new Southern Group. The Lancaster-Morecambe-Heysham lines, then in the London Midland & Scottish Group, continued to operate on 25Hz ac until 1953.

The major electrification event of the Grouping years was the extension of the Southern Railway's system over the main lines from London to Brighton, Eastbourne and Portsmouth, and along the South Coast from Portsmouth to Ore; accompanied by the widespread conversion of suburban and outer suburban routes which brought Reading in the west and Gillingham and Maidstone in the east into the Southern Electric network. Elsewhere in the country the pattern of electrification was irregular as far as the main line railways were concerned. In the London suburban area north of the Thames the LMS operated certain electric services and further afield there were electrified systems based on Manchester, Liverpool, Lancaster, and Newcastle upon Tyne.

In the years after World War II earlier experiments with using industrial frequency ac as a traction supply were resumed with fresh vigour on the Continent. Early hopes of developing a 50Hz traction motor competitive in size and simplicity with the long-established dc machine were not fully realised, however, but rectifiers suitable for installation in locomotives and motorcoaches were by this time available and so the solution generally adopted was a high-voltage supply at 50Hz to the contact wire, which was then transformed down and rectified on board the motive power to provide dc at a suitable voltage for the traction motors.

In the early 1950s British Railways still favoured dc electrification following the recommendations of several technical reports, but an experiment in 50Hz ac traction was undertaken on the Lancaster-Morecambe-Heysham lines where some ex-dc emus converted with rectifiers for ac operation began a public service in 1953. By this time two dc schemes which had been delayed by the war were in operation. Liverpool Street-Shenfield had been completed in 1949, with subsequent extensions to Chelmsford and Southend Victoria; The Manchester-Sheffield-Wath electrification had been inaugurated in stages and work was well advanced on the new Woodhead Tunnel, completion of which enabled through electric services between Manchester and Sheffield to be inaugurated on 14 September 1954. In the following year the British Railways Modernisation Plan was published and included proposals for further electrification of main lines and suburban routes. At the beginning of 1956 it was announced that the decision had been taken that new work outside the Southern Region should be on the 50Hz system at 25,000V (or 6,250V in urban areas where the necessary bridgework for the higher voltage would be very expensive); not only that, but the existing dc electrification out of Liverpool Street was to be converted to the 50Hz ac system. Manchester-Sheffield-Wath continued at 1,500V dc, as did the Manchester, South Junction & Altrincham line at first but after completion of the Euston main line electrification to Manchester and Liverpool it was converted to ac in 1971.

Since 1959 the BR standard high-voltage ac system has been brought into service as follows:

Colchester-Clacton-Walton (pilot scheme)	1959
Manchester-Crewe	1960

Liverpool Street-Chelmsford and Southend Victoria*	1960
Liverpool Street-Hertford East-Enfield Town-Chingford-Bishops Stortford	1960
Glasgow suburban (north of Clyde)	1960
Liverpool-Crewe	1961
Fenchurch Street-Shoeburyness (LT&S line)	1961-62
Chelmsford-Colchester	1962
Glasgow suburban (south of Clyde)	1962
Crewe-Euston (via Trent Valley)	1962-65
Stafford-Rugby via Birmingham, and Colwich-Stockport via Stoke-on-Trent	1966-67
Glasgow-Gourock-Wemyss Bay	1967
Lea Valley line (Clapton-Cheshunt)	1969
Manchester-Altrincham†	1971
Weaver Junction-Glasgow	1973-74
Moorgate-Hertford North-Welwyn Garden City	1976
Kings Cross-Hitchin-Royston	1977
Rutherglen-Kelvinhaugh (Argyle Line)	1979

* Conversion to ac. Electrified to Shenfield at 1,500V dc in 1949 and extended to Chelmsford and Southend Victoria on same system in 1956.

† Conversion to ac. Electrified at 1,500V dc in 1931.

The total electrified system of BR in 1979 comprised 2,310 route-miles of which 1,125 route-miles were high-voltage ac and 1,185 route-miles dc (71 route-miles at 1,500V overhead and 1,114 route-miles third rail).

In the standard BR 25kV ac system power is taken from the high-voltage Grid network of the Electricity Boards, usually at 132kV, at feeder stations spaced between 20 and 30 miles apart. In the Grid stations the voltage is stepped down in transformers to 25kV and fed to the trackside feeder stations and thence through circuit-breakers to the railway overhead system. Because the Grid is a three-phase system and the railway system is single-phase the phase connections at the feeder stations are chosen so as to minimise unbalance of the three-phase system. Supplies from the Grid must not be interconnected, so there is a break in the electrical continuity of the railway overhead system by a neutral section mid-way

Above: Ecclefechan feeder station, south of Lockerbie. Incoming supplies on right and outgoing feeders to the railway on left. BR

between feeder stations, at a 'mid-point track-sectioning cabin'. There are usually similar neutral sections at each feeder station, where as far as possible supplies are taken from two independent sources. These neutral sections also separate the adjacent supplies if a feeder station has to be switched out for maintenance and the load is taken by adjacent feeder stations. Switchgear is provided so that neutral sections can be bridged through busbars in the lineside installations if an interruption of supply makes it necessary to change the normal pattern of feeding.

The 'dead' section of contact wire at a neutral section is separated from the 'live' sections on each side of it by insulators which are of slightly larger cross-section than the wire, on which pantographs slide in exactly the same way as they run along the energised contact wire. The length of the 'dead' section is only 15ft (4.5m). At all neutral sections magnets similar to those of the automatic warning system (aws) are mounted on the sleeper. They open the circuit-breaker of a locomotive before it enters the neutral section, so that no current is being taken at the moment the pantograph leaves the energised wire, and re-close the circuit-breaker afterwards. This system is known as 'automatic power control' (apc). The 'dead' section of wire is earthed, so that if a train circuit-breaker did not open and an arc was drawn the lineside circuit-breakers would trip and the insulators would not be damaged.

Another type of insulator used in the overhead system, to be seen where there is point and crossing work, is the section insulator. While separating adjacent sections of contact wire, it does not interrupt the supply to the pantograph, being arranged so that the pantograph is continuously in electrical contact with one or the other section of energised wire.

At neutral sections where change of voltage between 25kV and 6.25kV takes place, equipment in the motive power unit sets up circuits appropriately for the voltage of the section being entered before the circuit-breaker re-closes. To enable new rolling stock to be 25kV only, the 6.25kV sections are being progressively eliminated. None had to be provided on the London Midland Region main line or elsewhere between Euston and Glasgow enabling all locomotives to be single-voltage. The remaining 6.25kV sections in Scotland on the Glasgow suburban lines north and south of the Clyde were converted to 25kV operation in 1979, and in the Eastern Region the Southend Victoria-Shenfield line had been converted and 25kV extended along the main lines towards Liverpool Street as far as Gidea Park, being programmed to reach Manor Park in 1980 and Liverpool Street in 1981. The longest surviving 6.25kV sections on the line from Liverpool Street, those on the Chingford, Enfield and Bishops Stortford routes; are planned for conversion in the early 1980s. Thus if electrification is extended to Cambridge train services on that main line could be hauled by standard 25kV locomotives. The final sections of 6.25kV working, Fenchurch Street-Barking and Leigh-Shoeburyness are planned for conversion to 25kV in the early 1980s.

Between feeder stations, track-sectioning cabins are provided at intervals, equipped with groups of circuit-breakers similar to those in the feeder stations. Connections are made through the circuit-breakers to common busbars which parallel the feeds to the tracks so that the load is evenly shared between them. All this switchgear operates automatically in case of faults and can also be opened by remote control to isolate sections of the overhead system for maintenance or in case of emergency. It would often be operationally inconvenient to isolate the whole length of line between groups of circuit-breakers and so intermediate hand-operated isolators are provided in the overhead system but these must only be opened or closed after the opening of the circuit-breakers on each side of them. After the isolators have been operated, the circuit-breakers are reclosed to restore power to the remainder of the section.

With the Weaver Junction-Glasgow electrification of 1973/4 and subsequent schemes it became general practice to install circuit-breakers in which the contacts are inside a sealed vacuum chamber. In these conditions the arc is extinguished after a contact separation of about half an inch. The contacts have a very long life and do not require the frequent routine inspections necessary with earlier circuit-breakers in which the contacts were inside a tank containing insulating oil which had to be lowered and then winched back into position at every inspection. In this older pattern the contacts opened to a gap of several inches. The vacuum type is called a 'vacuum interrupter'. It is quieter in operation and the mechanism is lighter and simpler. Vacuum interrupters have also been developed for roof mounting on locomotives and multiple-unit vehicles to replace the conventional air-blast circuit-breaker. With neutral sections occurring every ten miles or so, this piece of equipment has a much more severe duty than the circuit breaker in a fixed installation which normally operates only on faults or at maintenance periods. With the electric APT running at 125mile/h, its power car circuit-breakers would operate about every five minutes.

Switchgear over wide areas is monitored and controlled from Electrical Control Rooms where its condition (open or closed) is shown on a mimic diagram or the screens of visual display units (vdus). The rooms are continuously manned and it is from here that isolations for routine maintenance or to cope with an emergency are directed.

The catenary system from which trains collect power is erected in tension lengths of up to 6,000ft (1.8km). With modern main line equipment each full length is restrained at one or more structures in the middle and tensioned by weights at the ends. Adjacent lengths overlap so that the supply to the trains is unbroken. At overlaps the sections of catenary system may be directly connected together so as to be electrically continuous, or the connection may be taken through a hand-operated isolator of the type mentioned above and/or a booster transformer, provided for suppression of telecommunications interference. The overlap is then known as an 'insulated overlap' because of the insulation provided in the catenary and contact wire to ensure electrical separation of the conductors.

Various types of catenary system were used in the early stages of the BR electrification but by the time of the extension from Weaver Junction to Glasgow a design known as Mk IIIA had been developed. A similar design, slightly modified in some respects, was used for the Great Northern suburban schemes. The St Pancras/Moorgate-Bedford electrification is using a later version, Mk IIIB,

Below: 'Sagged' catenary and single-track cantilevers near Abington, West Coast main line. Note the return conductors on the off side of the masts.
BR

Fig 12 'Sagged' catenary (Mk IIIA)

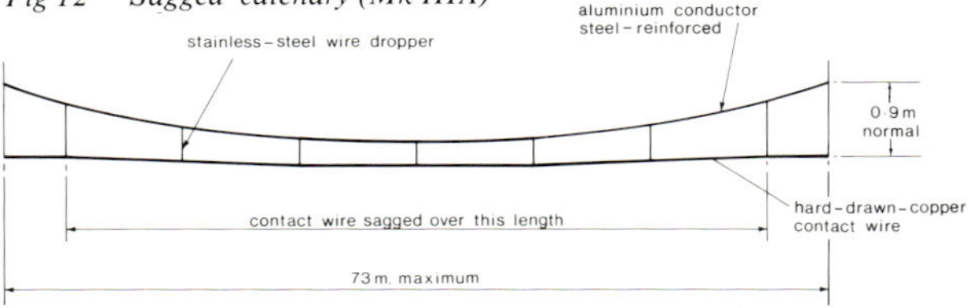

differing mainly in contact wire tension and the metrication of certain fittings. Some Mk IIIA equipment has been retensioned to Mk IIIB standards to combat windage and to improve performance for 125mile/h operation with APT.

Mk IIIA and IIIB are both simple catenary systems, ie the contact wire is suspended by droppers from a single catenary conductor as shown in Fig 12. This is a Mk IIIA span and it will be noted that in the maximum span length of 73m (240ft) illustrated there is a sag of 100mm (4in) in the contact wire at mid-span. In Mk IIIB the sag is 75mm (3in). The sag improves current collection at speed by presenting a substantially level contact wire to the uplifted pantograph. The wire lifts with the passage of a train and

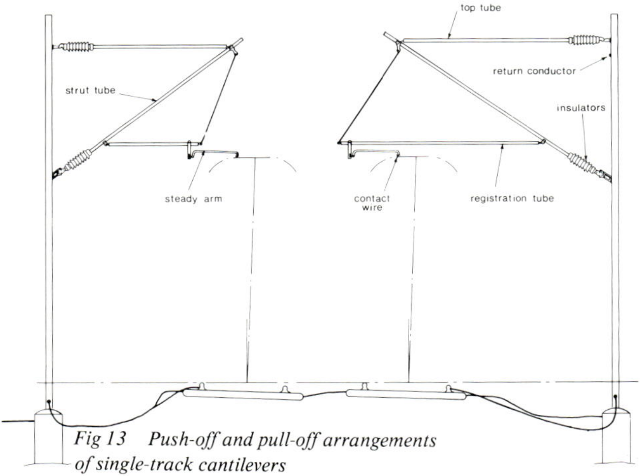

Fig 13 Push-off and pull-off arrangements of single-track cantilevers

the lift is greater at mid-span than at the supports. This is compensated by the sag.

The catenary consists of seven wires stranded together, two being Alumoweld wires (steel with a deposited coating of aluminium) and the others aluminium. This type of cable is called awac (Alumoweld/aluminium conductors). Droppers are of stainless steel wire and the contact wire is hard-drawn copper at 107sq mm (0.166sq in) cross-section.

The catenary on double-track sections is supported by separate masts for each track. Fig 13 shows the basic arrangement of masts and cantilevers. The contact wire does not follow the centre line of the track, but in order to spread the area of wear on the pantographs is staggered from side to side of it in each span, crossing the centre line in mid-span. On straight track the stagger is from 230mm (9in) off-centre at one mast to 230mm on the other side of the centre line at the next. On curves the stagger is increased up to 380mm (15in). The two methods of positioning the contact

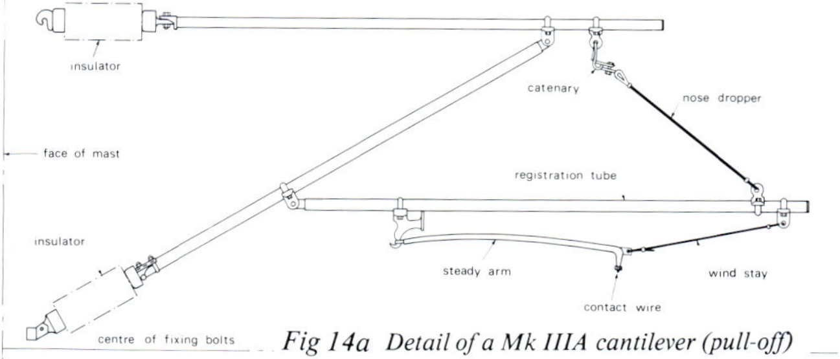

Fig 14a Detail of a Mk IIIA cantilever (pull-off)

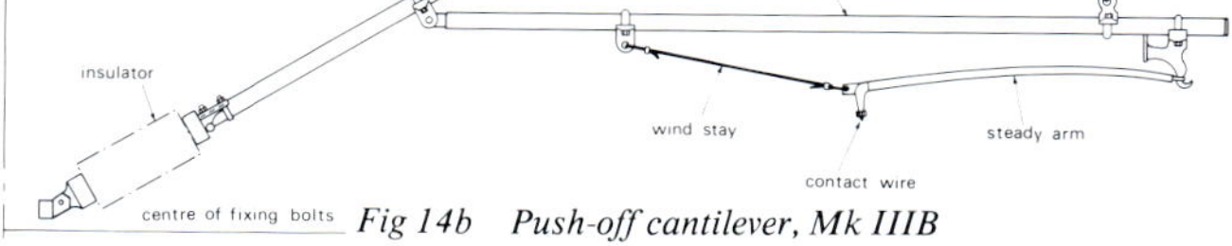

Fig 14b Push-off cantilever, Mk IIIB

wire over the track are shown in the diagram. The left-hand configuration is called 'pull-off' and the right-hand one 'push-off'. The two arrangements alternate on straight track. A Mk IIIB cantilever is shown in detail in Fig 14. The attachment of the top tube and the strut tube to the mast allows them to pivot in either direction as the catenary system expands or contracts with changing temperature.

Each mast is bonded to an adjacent running rail, the system being earthed through the foundations by virtue of all such connections in parallel. The return conductor near the top of the mast provides an insulated return path for the traction current which reduces electromagnetic interference in nearby telecommunication circuits from the effects of traction current. 'Booster' transformers' with one winding in series with the return conductor and the other in series with the contact wire are mounted at about 3.2km (2 mile) intervals on the lineside masts at insulated overlaps. Their effect is to produce a potential difference which encourages the return traction current to flow in the return conductor, which is connected to the running rail approximately mid-way between the booster transformers.

On four-track sections the headspan construction shown in Fig 15 is used. Except at the restraining structures at the centre of its length, the catenary cable is carried in the pulleys and the contact wire is located by a steady arm as before. The two cross-span wires below the headspan wire are copper-clad to carry fault current.

Current is collected from the overhead contact wire by a pantograph. The collector head is mounted at the top of a

Below: Overlap span with booster transformers mounted at the back of the masts. BICC

Above: Headspan construction at Winwick Junction, WCML. BR

collapsible framework which provides a reasonably constant upward force derived from springs. The pantograph is released and lowered by an air cylinder which overrides the springs. The collecting surface is formed by renewable strips of metal-impregnated carbon, which reduce wear of the contact wire compared with metal collectors and have a lubricating action on the wire.

Two main types of pantograph are seen on BR ac lines. One based on a Continental pattern, carries the collector on the upper of two jointed arms. The other is of the conventional 'diamond' pattern except that the lower members are crossed to give it a shorter base on the locomotive or multiple-unit vehicle roof.

The direct current lines take three-phase ac power from the Grid system and distribute it over their own lineside cables to substations, where the supply is stepped down in transformers to the traction

Fig 15 Headspan construction for four-track lines

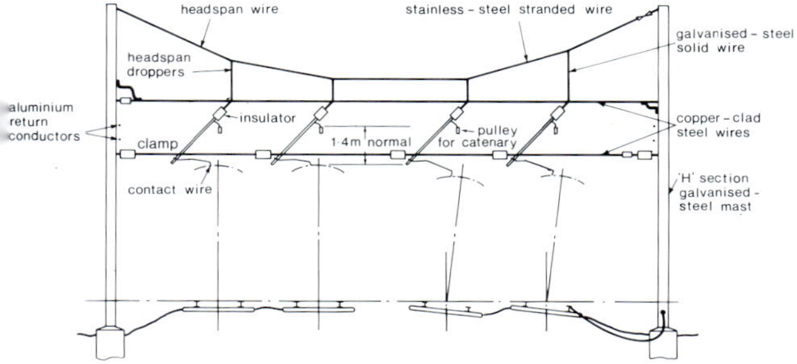

voltage and then rectified, so that direct current is fed to the trains. High-voltage cables are now generally oil-filled, which makes them less liable to internal breakdown than the old 'solid' type and enables them to work at a higher temperature, so that a cable of smaller cross-section can be used to carry a given maximum load. Vertical cylindrical reservoirs for the oil can be seen at intervals along the cable route, which is often in a trench covered with concrete slabs. Oil flows into the reservoirs when it expands with the heat of the cable, and returns when the cable cools.

Substation spacings on the lower-voltage (ie 750V and under) dc lines vary from under a mile in busy areas to nearly five miles in the country. On the Manchester-Sheffield-Wath 1,500V line the average spacing is 6.2 miles. Many mercury-arc rectifiers are still in operation at substations but in all new work silicon diodes are used and conversions to silicon take place as renewals become due.

The 'live' conductor rail is mounted on insulators outside the running rails. To complete the circuit the traction return current flows through the axles and wheels into the running rails and back to the substation. The London Transport Underground system uses the positive third rail and a negative fourth rail in the centre of the track. This enables traction current to be kept clear of the running rails, simplifying the arrangements for signalling track circuits. Also, a short circuit earth fault from, say, a positive rail to a cast iron segment of a tube tunnel does not cause a supply interruption since earthing the positive merely means that the negative rail becomes the full voltage (630V in this case) below earth potential. For similar reasons, and for compatability for inter running, certain LMR lines were electrified on the fourth-rail system; all have been converted to third rail, and the fourth rail is only retained on those sections where LT trains operate, and here it is electrically connected to the running rails.

The conductor rails for up and down tracks are generally fed through separate circuit-breakers from substations at each end of the section concerned. Midway between substations there is often a lineside track-paralleling hut and gaps in the conductor rails, which are bridged electrically by a busbar in the hut. High-speed circuit-breakers are included in the connections between the conductor rails and the busbar. They open automatically to cut off the supply in case of a fault, or can be opened from a control room when a section of line has to be isolated. There are similar circuit-breakers at substations, so that wherever a fault occurs there will be a circuit-breaker within a short distance which will 'trip' to give protection.

On the low-voltage dc lines current is collected from the conductor rails by means of cast iron shoes sliding on the top surface. In stock built before the 1960s the shoes were usually suspended by links from shoebeams mounted between the axleboxes, and contact pressure was provided by their weight. On the SR all gravity shoegear was replaced some years ago by the spring-loaded radial type. In more recent stock the shoes are carried by arms pivoted at their inner ends from the bogie frame by a rubber-bushed arrangement which provides additional pressure by the 'springiness' of the rubber. In this type of shoegear there is still a beam between the axle-boxes, but its purpose is to limit the up and down movement of the shoes.

On the Manchester-Bury 1,200V dc line the shoegear differs from both these arrangements. Here the conductor rail is protected on top and at the sides, but a gap is left in the protecting woodwork sufficient for a flat shoe projecting downwards from the bogie to make contact with the side of the conductor rail head. The shoe has a pivot mounting, and a spring pushing outwards at its upper end causes the lower end to be pressed inwards against the rail with a suitable contact pressure.

Control Systems

In all BR ac electric locomotives and emus the traction motors operate on direct current taken from silicon rectifiers. Voltage control by tap-changer still predominates but by the 1980s increasing numbers of emus and locomotives with thyristor control were coming into service. In thyristor systems the voltage is controlled smoothly instead of in steps as by a tap-changer. The thyristor can be thought of, in fact, as a silicon rectifier which is also an 'electronic tap', regulating the flow of direct current through it. Continuous 'stepless' control avoids the sudden change in tractive effort which occurs when a tap-changer advanced from tap to tap, and which may cause loss of adhesion on slippery rails. At the time of writing (1979) only one BR electric locomotive, No 87.101 *Stephenson* has been equipped with thyristor control, but the system is used in the electric Advanced Passenger Train (APT-P).

The usual arrangement in thyristor motive power is to have two 'mixed' bridge rectifier circuits, each having thyristors in two arms and diodes in the other two. From zero to half-voltage only one bridge rectifies, the thyristors in the second bridge being switched off. There is a path for current, however, through the diodes in two arms of that bridge, which are not called upon at this stage to rectify but simply allow the direct current from bridge 1 to flow through them to the traction motors in their normal conducting direction.

When bridge 1 is delivering its full voltage, corresponding to the centre tap of the transformer, the thyristors in bridge 2 are activated and begin to rectify. This bridge is connected between the centre tap and the high-voltage end of the transformer winding, and its output is added to that of bridge 1. The thyristors in bridge 2 are 'opened up' as before until at the end of the process the full traction voltage is applied to the motors. For maximum speed the motor fields may be weakened in the usual way, by tappings or diverter resistances, but in No 87.101 and in APT-P the traction motor field windings are not in series with the armature as in the usual arrangement but are excited separately through thyristor rectifiers which provide electronic control of field strength.

In a thyristor system the only conventional switchgear may be the main circuit-breaker, the motor contactors and the reverser, all other control functions being performed electronically.

Control systems in dc traction have the same function as in ac of raising the motor voltage from a low value at starting, to prevent excessive current, to the full value at which the motors are designed to operate. Normally this involves the use of resistances, which are cut out in steps as the train accelerates, and change of motor grouping from series to parallel at the half-voltage point. Field-weakening follows after full voltage has been reached.

It was once common to perform all dc control switching by individual electro-pneumatic contactors but it is now general practice to use camshafts to operate groups of switches which have to follow a particular sequence. The camshaft is often driven by an oil servo-motor with compressed air control. Resistance control wastes energy as heat while the resistances are in circuit, although the heat is in some cases used for train heating. Chopper control is an alternative to resistance control. This is an electronic system in which thyristors switch the motor current on and off very rapidly so that it flows in a series of pulses. Since the voltage across a circuit does not rise instantaneously to the full voltage of the supply, it can be controlled by switching off while it is at an intermediate value. To build up to full voltage either the pulse length or the pulse frequency is increased until the thyristors are conducting continuously. British Rail is experimenting with chopper control but no equipment of this type is yet in service on BR.

The Multiple-Unit System

Most traffic on the dc lines and many suburban and secondary services on the ac system are worked by electric multiple-unit trains (emus). A unit consists of one or more powered coaches (motorcoaches) and one or more trailers. When there is a single motorcoach in a unit it may be at one end of the formation and have a driving compartment, when the vehicle at the other end and will have to be a driving trailer with a driver's compartment containing the normal controls; if the motorcoach is marshalled intermediately, both end vehicles must be driving trailers. There are many varieties of unit formation. The most powerful units on BR are the Class 430s on the Southern Region which have a motorcoach at each end with all its axles motored, giving eight motors totalling 2,920hp in a four-coach unit. For operating with the Class 430s and certain other duties the Southern has a number of four-car trailer units (Class 491) which are not powered but have a driving trailer at each end for remote control of a Class 430 unit, a Class 33 diesel-electric locomotive, or a Class 73 electro-diesel.

The basis of the multiple-unit system is that units can be coupled together to form trains of various lengths in which the ratio of power to weight remains constant. Each unit has its own control and power equipment, but all respond to the movements of the driver's controller in the leading cab, the units being wired throughout with control cables which are interconnected between vehicles and between units by plug-in flexible 'jumpers'. The controller in an emu cab is therefore properly called a 'master controller' because it acts not only on the equipment of its own unit but of any other units coupled to it.

BR has standardised a four-position master controller for ac and dc stock, selecting the following conditions of running on the two systems:

ac

(1) Motors fed from lowest-voltage transformer tapping. Used for shunting movements.

(2) Motors at half-voltage.
(3) Motors at full voltage.
(4) Motor fields weakened for maximum speed.

dc

(1) Motors in series, all resistance in circuit. Used for shunting movements and must only be held for short periods to avoid overheating the resistances.
(2) Motors in series, all resistance cut out. Can be held continuously for slow-speed running.
(3) Motors in parallel, all resistance cut out. The motors are now running at their full rated voltage and the notch may be held continuously.
(4) Weak-field. As (3) but motor fields weakened for maximum speed. In the dc case a step called 'transition' takes place automatically between steps (2) and (3) in which the motors are switched from series to parallel and resistance is reinserted in the circuit. The short-circuiting of resistances to achieve the final states (2) and (3) is automatic, under the control of an accelerating relay, and field-weakening is initiated similarly if the driver has called for it by putting his controller in position (4). In some equipments the automatic cutting out of resistance in steps (2) and (3) can be arrested by moving the controller back to position (1) but this manoeuvre is only allowed in special circumstances, such as severe wheelslip, and the train must not run continuously in this condition because some resistance remains in circuit. It is often the practice when starting under clear signals and without speed restrictions to place the controller at once in position (4), allowing the train to accelerate under its automatic control.

In ac emus all four controller positions, or any intermediate settings of the tap-changer when these are available, can be used continuously.

In the Southern Region, multiple-unit control has been extended to cover control of different types of motive power from the standard type of emu controller. This facility is used for working trains from Weymouth to Bournemouth which are propelled by a Class 33/1 diesel-electric locomotive and driven from the cab of the leading driving trailer.

If an electro-diesel or a Class 33/1 locomotive is heading a train, any emu equipments in the formation can be controlled from its cab. By this system 'mixed power' trains can be operated, eg a Class 33/1 diesel-electric with trailer coaches combined with an emu.

Since 1976 a new 'hybrid' type of emu has been operating on BR. These are the Class 313 units on the GN Suburban electrification running between Welwyn Garden City, Hertford North, and Moorgate, which change between 25kV ac overhead and 750V dc third rail at Drayton Park, the latter system being used in the tunnel section between Drayton Park and Moorgate. These trains have a conventional dc control system with resistances and series/parallel motor groupings which is used both on ac and dc. There is no tap-changer, the transformer supplying a fixed 750V to the rectifiers when running on 25kV ac. In the tunnel section the transformer and rectifiers are switched out, the dc supply being collected direct from the third rail.

Electric Locomotives

The most numerous electric locomotives on BR are those operating on the West Coast main line and its associated routes. Classes 81 to 85 are survivors of the five prototype classes built for the early stages of this electrification; Class 86 followed in 1965, embodying ideas gained from experience with its predecessors; and Class 87 appeared in 1974 in readiness for the extension of electrification from Weaver Junction to Glasgow. These seven classes were the first electric locomotives on BR designed for a normal maximum speed of 100mile/h, and Classes 81 to 85 incorporated different types of flexible drive between the fully-springborne traction motors and the axles. It was later considered that the flexible drives were unnecessary and so the motors in Class 86 were axle-hung. Experience showed, however, that the track suffered from the unsprung weight when carrying a frequent high-speed service, and Class 87 saw a return to fully-springborne motors, but with a new British design of flexible drive replacing the Continental patterns used in the prototype classes.

When a motor is fully-springborne, ie supported wholly by the bogie frame, the distance between its armature shaft and the axle is constantly varying by a small amount with the action of the springs. The two cannot therefore be geared directly together as in an axle-hung arrangement, where one side of the motor frame is supported

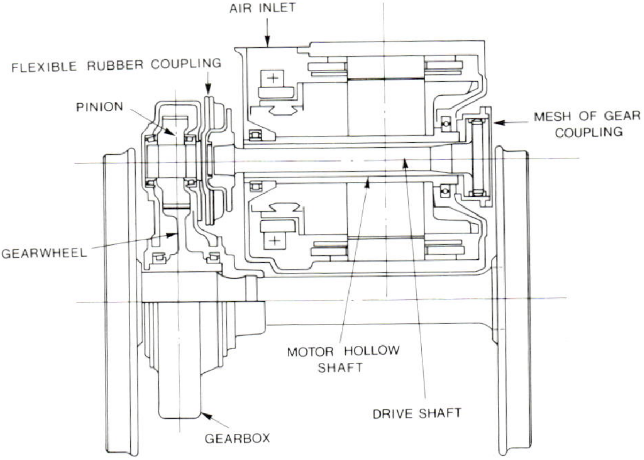

Fig 16 Flexible drive from traction motor to axle in a Class 87 locomotive

by bearings on the axle. In Class 87 the motor pinion and the axle gearwheel are at fixed centres in a gearcase supported by an axle bearing at one side and from the bogie frame at the other. The pinion is not mounted directly on the armature shaft but is driven by a cardan shaft which passes through a 'tunnel' at the centre of the armature with sufficient clearance to allow up and down movement. At one end the shaft is coupled to the armature by a gear type coupling which allows both radial and axial movement, and at the other end to the separate pinion shaft by a universal joint (Fig 16).

In the Class 86 locomotives an equipment layout was adopted which grouped the power equipment for individual motors, comprising rectifier, motor blower, smoothing choke and switchgear, in blocks located above each bogie. The same principle was followed in Class 87 (Fig 17). Rheostatic braking was fitted from Class 85 (the first locomotive built with semiconductor rectifiers instead of mercury-arcs) onwards.

After the LMR electrics, the next most numerous electric locomotives on BR are the Southern Region's electro-diesels of Classes 73/0 and 73/1. The idea of a dual-power locomotive able to operate away from the live rail or through sections where power is cut off for maintenance, goes back to Southern Railway days. Early

Fig 17 Class 87 locomotive equipment layout **1**—*Pantograph.* **2**—*Pantograph air motor.* **3**—*Air-blast circuit-breaker.* **4**—*HT connections.* **5**—*Main transformer.* **6**—*HT tap-changer.* **7**—*Input bushing.* **8**—*Transformer oil pump.* **9**—*Transformer radiator.* **10**—*Conservator (transformer oil).* **11**—*Brake resistor No 1.* **12**—*Brake resistor No 2.* **13-16**—*Main rectifiers Nos 1 to 4.* **17**—*Surge diverter.* **18-21**—*Smoothing chokes Nos 1 to 4.* **22-25**—*Traction motors Nos 1 to 4.* **26-29**—*Traction motor blowers Nos 1 to 4.* **30**—*Battery box.* **31**—*Battery charger.* **32**—*Auxiliary compressor.* **33**—*Main compressor.* **34**—*Auxiliary compressor.* **35-38**—*Control equipment frames Nos 1 to 4.* **39-40**—*Air equipment frames Nos 1 and 2.* **41**—*Main air reservoir.* **42**—*AWS receiver.* **43**—*Reservoir (2), brake supply.* **44**—*Weak-field and rheostatic brake equipment.* **45**—*Horns.*

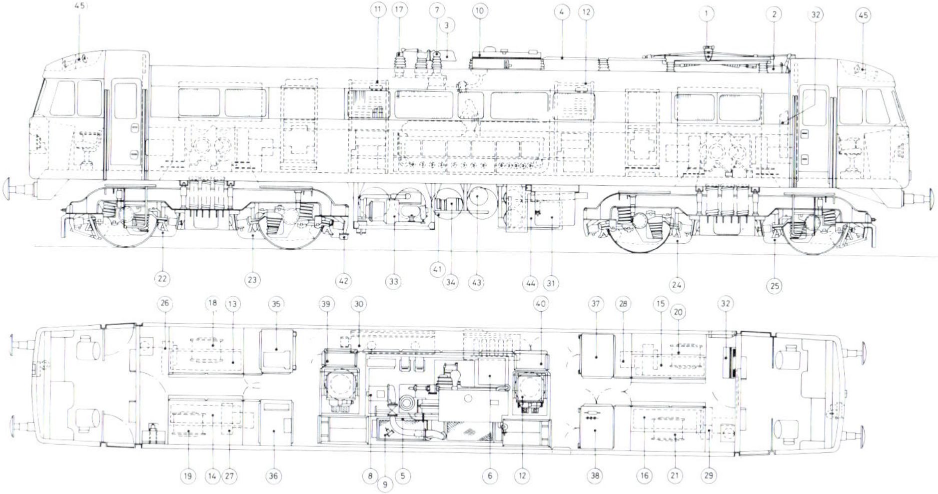

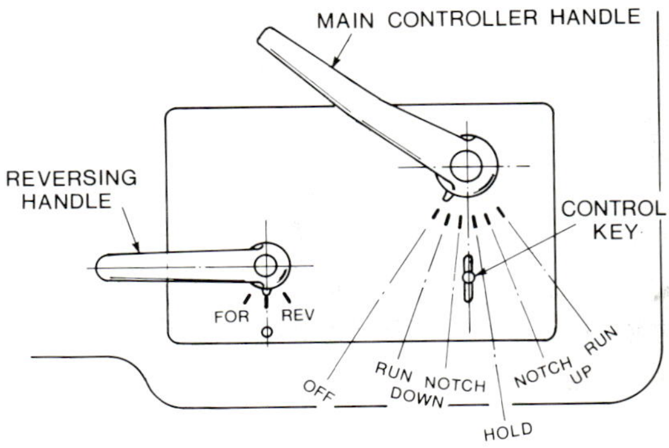

Fig 18 The standard driver's control arrangement for ac electric locomotives

proposals were for electric and diesel installations of similar power but this was found impracticable. In the two series of Class 73 locomotives the electric rating is 1,600hp and the diesel rating 600hp.

The number of Class 76 locomotives on the Manchester-Sheffield-Wath electrification is shrinking and the future of the route is uncertain. Some notes on this classic 1,500V dc design are given in the section on individual classes.

Locomotive Controls (ac)

From the beginning of ac locomotive traction on BR it was the policy to give the driver full control of acceleration. The standard locomotive controller throughout the ac fleet is illustrated in Fig 18. The main controller faceplate is divided into 'down' and 'up' sectors, each with 'notch' and 'run' positions. There is a 'hold' position between the two sectors. Before the controller handle can be moved from 'off', 'forward' or 'reverse' must be selected with the adjacent reverser handle, and this in turn is locked in the mid-position until released by inserting and operating a removable control key. Similar control locking arrangements apply to nearly all motive power, including emus, built since 1952.

The later (Class 87) locomotives are fitted with a driver's vigilance system. While driving, a two-position pedal has to be depressed. After 60sec an audible signal begins, and if the pedal is

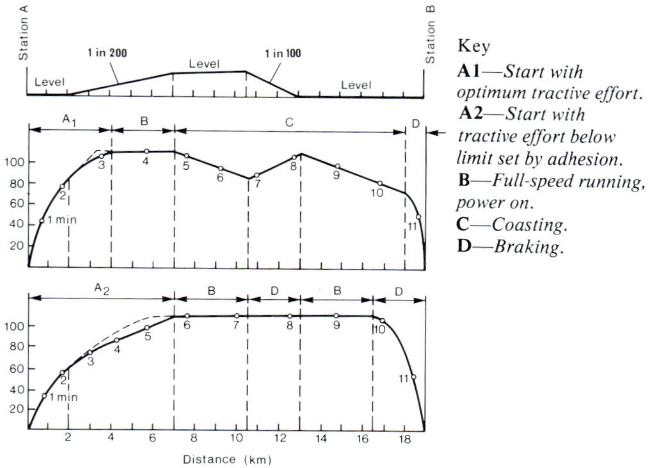

Fig 19 Driving techniques compared

not released and depressed again an emergency brake application is made after a further 5-7sec. The system can be reset at any time during the cycle convenient to the driver. Resetting the aws equipment after a 'warning' signal also resets the vigilance system. A desk-mounted hand switch is also provided for the same purpose.

In starting a train the controller may be moved to and fro between 'notch' and 'hold' in the 'up' sector, causing the tap changer to notch up one step at a time; or the handle may be set at 'run up' and returned to 'hold' as necessary to maintain a steady accelerating current. In either case the driver watches the ammeters and manipulates the controller to keep the pointers in the yellow sectors of their scales.

A notch indicator shows the proportion of full voltage being applied to the motors as the tap-changer notches up. If speed continues to rise after full voltage has been reached the locomotive goes into weak-field automatically and the notch indicator pointer enters the weak-field sector of its scale.

A skilful driver can do much to save energy while still keeping to the timetable. Two driving methods over a hypothetical section between two stations 19km apart are compared in Fig 19. In diagram (a) the driver notches up quickly to full power and attains maximum speed for the section after 4km while climbing the 1 in 200 gradient. Speed is still rising, but by notching back he holds it steady and on reaching the top of the bank he cuts power off and starts coasting. Speed falls slightly over the level stretch but recovers on the subsequent falling gradient of 1 in 100. Coasting continues over the next level section, with the train decelerating until the brakes are applied at 18km to stop at station B. The journey of 19km has taken the scheduled 12min although the locomotive was only drawing power for the first 7km.

Diagram (b) shows a less confident start in which line speed is only reached after 7km. Time has already been lost and the driver keeps power on to maintain speed over the level section. On the subsequent falling gradient he has to brake to keep to the limit and useful kinetic energy is wasted as heat. On the level he notches up again to maintain speed and at 16.5km begins braking from full speed in order to stop at Station B. The 12 min schedule has been observed but the locomotive has drawn power from the overhead line for 14 of the 19km and there has been greater waste of energy and more mechanical wear and tear in braking.

Locomotive Controls (dc)

Throughout their long life the Class 76 locomotives on the 1,500V dc Manchester-Sheffield-Wath electrification represented the classic methods of dc locomotive control, with step-by-step notching and a separate 'combination lever' operated by the driver to change from series to parallel motor grouping. These locomotives were fitted from the first for regenerative braking, and the driver had to balance the regenerated voltage with the voltage in the overhead line before allowing regeneration to begin. At a later stage rheostatic braking was added, but this was blended with the ordinary braking system and only required operation of a switch to bring it into action.

The design of the Manchester-Sheffield-Wath locomotives dated from before World War II and by the time they became operational the use of motor-driven camshaft controllers was growing elsewhere. With these it was possible to provide 'hold', 'notch' and 'run' positions for the driver's control handle, corresponding to those in the ac locomotives, although usually with the restriction that only certain notches could be used continuously. The first BR electric locomotives with this form of control were the Class 71s which were unusual in that they incorporated a motor-generator system with the control acting on the generator excitation instead of on resistances in the main power circuit. Consequently all notches could be used continuously.

In the present Southern Region electro-diesels there is similar provision in electric working for step-by-step notching or for 'running up', but in this case the progression is controlled by a relay. Four weak-field notches can be used in either grouping. Transition from series to parallel is automatic in both electric and diesel modes of operation.

BR ac Locomotives

Classes 81 to 85, as mentioned earlier, are the five prototype designs built for the initial stages of the LMR electrification. They were supplied by various firms to a common performance specification which called for:

a—Hauling a 475 ton trailing express passenger load from Manchester (London Road, now Piccadilly) to London (Euston) with a balancing speed of 90mile/h on level tangent track and a maximum running speed of 100mile/h. Average speed to be 67mile/h with one stop of 1min and 4 miles at 15mile/h additional speed restrictions for track maintenance.
b—Hauling a 950 ton freight train between Manchester (Longsight) and London (Willesden) at an average speed of 42mile/h with a maximum speed of 55mile/h; also 500 ton freight trains (fully fitted) over this section at a maximum speed of 60mile/h. The locomotive also had to be capable of making three consecutive starts with the 950 ton train up to 20mile/h on a 1 in 100 gradient, and of working without damage to the equipment with this train for 10 miles at 10mile/h on any part of this route (this was to ensure no harm would come from long periods of very slow running in dense fog).

Further requirements were that the maximum axle-load should be 20 tons and the minimum wheel diameter 48in. All locomotives were to have flexible drives in order to minimise unsprung weight.

Individual differences between the classes are mentioned under the respective headings, but all were of Bo-Bo wheel arrangement. Classes 81 to 84 had mercury-arc rectifiers of various kinds; locomotives of Class 85 were the first on BR with semiconductor rectifiers (although some emus were already so equipped). In later years all the mercury-arc rectifiers were replaced with silicon diodes.

Originally all these classes were equipped with two pantographs. Normally the trailing one was raised in accordance with the general practice of the time, which held that if the pantograph in use were damaged by an obstruction the leading one would have passed harmlessly underneath and could be raised in its place. By the time Class 86 was designed, however, it was decided that the use made of the second pantograph in these circumstances was not high enough to justify carrying two, and all classes now carry only one.

Flexible drives and air-blast circuit-breakers of designs already well proven on the Continent were specified for all locomotives of the first five classes.

The following notes describe the locomotives as built. Apart from the substitution of silicon rectifiers throughout, the other features remain unchanged in locomotives of the various classes still in service. One of the electrical equipment suppliers for the prototype locomotives was Associated Electrical Industries Ltd (AEI), an amalgamation of the former Metropolitan-Vickers Electrical Co Ltd, based at Manchester, and the British Thomson-Houston Co Ltd, which had its headquarters at Rugby. The two parts of the organisation are referred to in the notes as AEI (Manchester) and AEI (Rugby). Both are now merged with The General Electric Co Ltd as GEC Traction Ltd.

Class 81

The first ac electric locomotive to appear was No 3001 (now 81.001) which was handed over to BR in 1959. It belonged to a

Below: With the environment in mind, an exceptionally unobtrusive insulator was designed for cantilevers on the Tyne & Wear Metro.
NEI Parsons

Above: As No 3001 of Class AL1, No 81.001 was the first of the ac electric locomotives to be handed over to the London Midland Region. Here the veteran pulls away from Rugby on a down parcels train. P. Grand

series of 25 built by AEI (Rugby), with mechanical parts built by the Birmingham Railway Carriage & Wagon Co Ltd. The rectifiers were three multi-anode tanks of basically industrial design but modified to minimise splashing of the mercury pool. Control was by cam-operated contactors on the low-tension side of the transformer. The locomotives had Alsthom type bogie pivots consisting of a vertical column with conical rubber bearings in the underframe and in the fixed bolster of each bogie. Tractive effort was transmitted through the column, the rubber allowing pivoting and lateral movements, the latter controlled by springs. Body weight was borne partly by the columns and partly by the side bearers. The flexible drive was also an Alsthom system, the motors being geared to quill shafts from which torque was transmitted to the road wheels through rubber-bushed links.

Weight: 78 tons 3cwt
Wheel dia: 4ft 0in
Length over buffers: 56ft 6in
Rating: 3,200 rail hp

Class 82

Ten locomotives were supplied by AEI (Manchester), with mechanical parts by Beyer, Peacock & Co Ltd. They had similar rectifiers to Class 81, but a high-tension tap-changer with chain-

Above: Class 82 No 82.002 was one of a batch of 10 built by Beyer, Peacock. Eric Bullen

driven sliders moving over fixed contacts in synchronism with the operation of three cam-operated switches. The bogies were a development of the design used in the Metropolitan-Vickers gas turbine locomotive, the pivot pin projecting downwards from a fixed transom. A 'spring cap' resting on coil springs on the transom corresponded to the conventional bolster. Swing links at each end of the spring caps carried a beam forming part of the body structure, which passed under the bogie frame and on which the seating for the lower end of the pivot pin was mounted. Rubber-bushed links anchored the spring cap relative to the bogie frame and permitted lateral movement of the pivot seating. The arrangement was intended to provide the advantages of a conventional swing bolster without the wear of rubbing metal parts. Alsthom flexible drive was fitted.

Weight: 78 tons 10cwt
Wheel dia: 4ft 0in
Length over buffers: 56ft 0in
Rating: 3,300 rail hp

Class 83

The English Electric Co Ltd and its Vulcan Foundry works built 14 locomotives equipped initially with single-anode ignitron rectifiers. The fifteenth locomotive of the order was similar mechanically but from the outset had a silicon rectifier and a transductor system acting in conjunction with the tap-changer to provide stepless voltage control and automatic acceleration at a pre-set tractive effort. The transductors were later removed but the scheme foreshadowed the facilities which have since become available with thyristors. The bogies of this class had bolsters controlled by links instead of friction plates, and spring beams connected to the bolster by transverse links carried the secondary springing, replacing the conventional spring plank arrangement. Brown-Boveri spring drives transmitted the driving torque. Each motor supported a short quill shaft carrying a gearwheel with spring-loaded pads around its circumference which engaged with a 'spider' on the driving axle.

All locomotives had low-tension tap-changing with an air-operated camshaft controlling electro-pneumatic contactors in the power circuit. A feature exclusive to these locomotives was the use of three-phase motors for certain auxiliary drives. The machines were fed from the output from an Arno converter which, while running as a single-phase motor and driving a dc generator, also generated a three-phase supply.

Weight: 75 tons 4cwt
Wheel dia: 4ft 0in
Length over buffers: 52ft 6in
Rating: 2,950hp

Below: No 83.014 of Class 83. This is another of the 'originals' and with its sister locomotives differed from the rest in the use of three-phase motors for certain auxiliary drives. Eric Bullen

Above: First of the early classes to suffer extensive withdrawals was Class 84. No 84.008 waits at Euston to run light to Willesden.
R. G. Budgen

Class 84

For the 10 locomotives it supplied in conjunction with the North British Locomotive Co Ltd. The General Electric Co Ltd developed a special single-anode mercury-arc rectifier known as the 'Com-Pak', aimed at combining desirable features of the ignitron and the excitron in a form specifically suitable for traction. The high-tension tap-changer was basically an electric motor-driven camshaft. Control was pneumatic, the shaft being locked in each position by air-operated pawls which also made and broke the feed to the camshaft motor as each notch was taken. Bogies were a conventional swing bolster design with oil-immersed side bearers but the traction forces were transmitted by rubber-bushed links. The flexible drives were similar to those in Class 83.

Weight: 75 tons 7cwt
Wheel dia: 4ft 0in
Length over buffers: 53ft 6.5in
Rating: 3,100 rail hp

Class 85

Class 85 was transitional. BR had already adopted semiconductor rectifiers for the Class 304 emus and now applied them to locomotives. Silicon diodes with characteristics suitable for traction were becoming available and promised to supplant germanium earlier than had been expected. A cautious start was made with this

Above: The 40 locomotives of Class 85 were built by BR and were the first to be equipped with semiconductor rectifiers, at first either germanium or silicon, but now all have been converted to silicon. The diodes occupied less space than the mercury-arc rectifiers originally fitted in the other four 'pilot' classes and enabled rheostatic braking to be provided. No 85.005 was photographed at Crewe. Barry J. Nicolle

material, 10 locomotives of the class being equipped with silicon rectifiers and the other 30 with germanium but these were later converted to silicon as well. Electrical equipment was supplied by AEI (Rugby) and apart from some circuit changes and the addition of rheostatic braking was generally similar to Class 81 except for the rectifiers. The locomotives were built by BR, 20 at Doncaster and 20 at Crewe, and had similar bogies and flexible drives to Class 81. Originally the rheostatic brake was controlled by the power handle after operating a power/brake changeover switch but the class was later modified to coordinate rheostatic braking with operation of the driver's automatic brake valve.

Weight: 81 tons 3cwt
Wheel dia: 4ft 0in
Length over buffers: 56ft 6in
Rating: 3,200 rail hp

Class 86

Designed on the basis of experience with the prototype locomotives, Class 86 dispensed with flexible drives and simplified the control equipment by omitting weak-field notches. Being introduced in

1965, after 25kV had been approved for the whole of the LMR main line electrification, no provision was made for 6.25kV working. The high-tension tap-changer was a development of that used in Class 82. Silicon rectifiers were installed in all the 100 locomotives of the class, and rheostatic braking was combined with the locomotive air/vacuum brake control. English Electric and AEI were jointly responsible for the electrical equipment. Mechanical design was by BR, 40 locomotives being built at Doncaster and 60 at the Vulcan Foundry works of English Electric. The bogie frames were supported by coil springs on equalising beams underslung from the axleboxes. Pivoting was by double-ended cone rubber assembly similar to that in Classes 81 and 85. In practice the use of axle-hung motors in high-speed intensive traffic proved hard on the track and the riding of the locomotives left something to be desired.

Above left: Class 86/0 No 86.033 is fitted for multiple-unit working but retains the original type of suspension. Barry J. Nicolle

Left: The Flexicoil suspension now fitted to all locomotives of Class 86/2 is seen in this picture of 86.210. Geoff Pinder

Above: Two Class 86/2 locomotives pass near Rugby. No 86.261 in the foreground heads the 10.55 Euston-Manchester. Philip D. Hawkins

Experiments were therefore carried out with Flexicoil suspension, which is now fitted to all locomotives classified as 86/2. The motors are still axle-hung but the load on the track has been relieved by fitting SAB resilient wheels. Class 86/0 has retained the original suspension and in passenger service has been confined as far as possible to duties not requiring continuous 100mile/h running, but this series is also to be equipped with SAB wheels. Three locomotives were fitted with bogies and fully springborne traction motors of the type built for the subsequent Class 87 and are classified 86/1. Ten 86/2 locomotives have the 'crossed-arm' pantograph which was later initially fitted throughout Class 87.

Weight: 86/0 81 tons 10cwt/82 tons 11cwt
86/1 85 tons 8cwt
86/2 83 tons 13cwt/84 tons 11cwt
Wheel dia: 3ft 9in
Length over buffers: 58ft 6in
Ratings: 86/0 36,000 rail hp
86/1 5,000 rail hp
86/2 4,040 rail hp

Class 87/0

To provide additional motive power for West Coast main line services to Scotland, 35 Class 87/0 locomotives were introduced from 1973. A 36th similar locomotive was fitted with thyristor control and is classified 87/1 (see below). All were built at Crewe by British Rail Engineering Ltd and supplied with electrical equipment by GEC Traction Ltd. This was the first 5,000hp locomotive class on BR. It marked a return to fully-springborne motors and field-weakening, but the flexible drive differed from that in Classes 81 to 85 in that the flexibility was between the motor and the pinion instead of between the gearwheel and the road wheels (see p000). The traction motors had compensating windings to improve commutation in weak-field conditions. Control in the 87/0 locomotives was by a high-tension tap-changer similar to the design used in Classes 82 and 86 but incorporating further improvements. The class is equipped for multiple-unit control and was the first on BR to provide air-braking only. The 'crossed-arm' pantograph first used on 10 Class 86 locomotives is fitted to all the 87s. Visually, the class is distinguished from its forerunners by having two front cab windows instead of three, and a central headlight between the two marker light units. In view of their use over the long gradients of the West Coast main line the locomotives are fitted with sanding gear as well as having a BR electronic system for controlling wheelspin.

Below: Class 87 was introduced in readiness for the electrification extension to Glasgow. No 87.013 at Springs Branch (Wigan) carries its John o' Gaunt *nameplates.* Eric Bullen

Sanding has also been fitted retrospectively in Class 86. Rheostatic braking is combined with the air brake control as in Class 86. The locomotive body is carried on the bogies by Flexicoil secondary suspension, traction and braking forces being transmitted through the kingpin connecting the body with the centre transom of the bogie. The kingpin is held in the transom by two laminated rubber buffers which allow transverse and rotational movements of the body relative to the bogie.

Class 87/1

The thyristor locomotive, No 87.101, is similar mechanically to the others of the class but weighs 4 tons less. Driving controls are also of the standard pattern and can be handled in the same way as when operating a tap-changer, but the driver can also select an 'advanced' mode in which he uses the controller handle to preset an appropriate tractive effort, additional markings being provided for this purpose. He can also preset a speed on a separate control. Moving the handle to position 1 closes the motor contactors to start the train and provides tractive effort suitable for handling a light locomotive. Further movement of the handle effects a stepless increase of tractive effort up to the desired level, which is then held until the selected speed is attained after which the motors run on their natural characteristic (ie tractive effort decreasing with speed). If maximum voltage is attained before the set speed, acceleration continues on

Below: Class 87/1 No 87.101, the thyristor-controlled locomotive which formed a class of its own, heads the down 'Royal Scot' at Greenholm. The locomotive is named Stephenson. D. E. Canning

Above: Driver's controls and instruments in a Class 87 locomotive.

the natural characteristic. The traction motor fields are separately excited through additional thyristor rectifiers which serve to control field strength during traction and when the rheostatic brake is in use.

	Class 87/0	*Class 87/1*
Weight:	81 tons 19cwt	77 tons 17cwt
Wheel dia:	1,150mm (3ft 9.25in)	1,150mm (3ft 9.25in)
Length over buffers:	58ft 6in	58ft 6in
Rating:	5,000rail hp	4,850rail hp

BR Locomotives (dc)

Classes 73/0 and 73/1

Deliveries of six prototype electro-diesel locomotives for the Southern Region began in 1961. These are Class 73/0. A further series of 43 with some detail modifications appeared between 1965 and 1967 and are now classified 73/1. This is a Bo-Bo design with a

Above: Far from the live rail, Class 73/1 No 73.135 uses its diesel power in piloting Class 33 No 33.110 on a coal train for Didcot, seen on Reading West curve. D. E. Canning

Top: The pivoted shoegear of a Class 73 is lowered on to the live rail. BR

1,600hp electrical equipment for 750V and a 600hp auxiliary diesel-electric installation. Its purpose has been described as 'to render the electrification of freight sidings unnecessary and to maximise the use of the fixed power supply equipment on a completely electrified railway by replacing conventional diesel-electric locomotives for all duties which cannot be performed with multiple-unit trains.' The auxiliary diesel power also overcomes the problem of stalling on conductor rail gaps which led to the use of booster control systems in earlier Southern electric locomotives. The equipment for live rail operation is a conventional series/parallel system with 20 resistance notches in series and 10 in parallel, and four weak-field steps available in each grouping. Ventilation apertures in the side walls and roof create a funnel effect which provides a strong flow of cooling air over the resistances while the locomotive is in motion. The driver can notch up step by step or let the equipment run up under the control of an accelerating relay. In Class 73/1 positions corresponding to the four notches of the standard emu controller are marked on the electric controller for use when running in multiple with emu stock. In diesel operation the engine speed is continuously variable and generator excitation is controlled by a load regulator, which also initiates transition. Changeover between electric and diesel power can be effected without stopping the locomotive. The collector shoes are lowered by an air engine when electric operation is selected, and raised by springs when the diesel set is in use.

	Class 73/0	*Class 73/1*
Weight:	75 tons 2cwt	75 tons 12cwt
Wheel dia:	3ft 4in	3ft 4in
Length over buffers:	53ft 8in	53ft 8in
Rating:	1,600hp electric (1,420rail hp) 600hp diesel (420rail hp)	1,600hp electric (1,420rail hp) 600hp diesel (420rail hp)
Gear ratio:	63:17	61:19
Max speed:	80mile/h	83/90mile/h

Class 76

Work on the 1,500V dc Manchester-Sheffield-Wath electrification was put in hand before World War II and the first of the 58 mixed traffic locomotives, whose survivors now form Class 76, was completed in 1941. This is a Bo+Bo design, tractive effort being transmitted through the bogies, which carry the buffing and drawgear and are coupled by an articulated joint. Series and series-parallel motor groupings with four weak-field steps in each provide

Above: Two Class 76 1,500V dc electric locomotives head westwards with coal for Fidlers Ferry power station from the Yorkshire coalfield via Wath yard. Barry J. Nicolle

10 economical running speeds. Notching, transition and regenerative braking are all controlled manually by the driver. Rheostatic braking was added in 1959. Later, some locomotives were fitted with larger compressors for working air-braked trains, while retaining their exhausters for vacuum-braked stock, and were also equipped for multiple-working in pairs. In more recent conversions the vacuum equipment has been removed when the compressor and multiple-unit modifications were carried out. The class has won a high reputation for reliability and in their later years the intervals between inspections and major maintenance were actually increased. An important modification among others leading to this result was the replacement of brass surfaces in the inter-bogie coupling by Ferrobestos, which greatly reduced wear.

Weight: 86 tons 14cwt/87 tons 14cwt
Wheel dia: 4ft 2in
Length over buffers: 50ft 6in
Rating: 1,300 rail hp

Electric Multiple-Units

For half a century the passenger services provided by electric traction in Great Britain were local or medium-distance. Frequent trains and short turn-rounds made multiple-unit operation ideal, and all electrified passenger lines adopted it. The following notes outline the development of emus (electric multiple-units) on BR since Nationalisation. Full details of unit formations, passenger capacity and accommodation, etc, are given in the Ian Allan abc pocket reference books, *BR Locomotives* and *BR Multiple Units*, and in the combined volume listing both electric and diesel motive power, all of which appear annually.

Southern Region

Up to the end of the 1970s most Southern Region commuter services were worked by four-car or two-car units generally similar to those introduced in the aftermath of World War II. Four-coach units had a motorcoach with driving compartment at each end and two intermediate trailers; the two-car units consisted of a motorcoach and driving trailer. Motorcoaches in both types were powered by two 250hp motors in one bogie. Similar formations were used in the main line and stopping train stock built for the first stage of the Kent Coast electrification of 1959 and subsequently (Classes 410/1 and 2; 411/1, 2 and 3; and 414/2 and 3), but in Classes 410/2, 411/2, 411/3 and 414/3 camshaft control was introduced in place of individual contactors. A four-year programme of refurbishing the Class 410 and 411 units began in August 1978. Improvements include new seating and interior panelling, improved lighting and heating, double-glazing and a public address system.

A change of practice occurred in the 'Brighton Replacement' stock of 1963 (Classes 420/1 and 421/1). In these units the end vehicles are driving trailers and the non-driving motorcoach is an intermediate vehicle. The motorcoach is powered by four 250hp motors, with the two motors in each bogie permanently in parallel, control being by series and parallel connection of the two pairs. Current is collected by shoes on the driving trailers. A similar

Below: Class 423 unit No 7728 leaves Gatwick Airport station for Three Bridges. Les Bertram

formation was adopted for the Class 423 four-car units introduced for the Bournemouth electrification of 1967 and since built in considerable numbers. Certain Class 423 units have been modified to provide additional luggage space for use on Victoria-Gatwick Airport services and are classified 427.

The four-coach Bournemouth express units of Class 430 are a special case in that the two motorcoaches are each powered by four 365hp motors. Collector shoes are carried on the motorcoaches — four on each side — and are interconnected through the unit in such a way that the last shoe to leave the conductor rail at a gap never breaks the circuit of more than four motors.

Replacement of life-expired Southern commuter stock began with the first deliveries in 1979 of Class 508 four-car units. This stock has two driving motorcoaches per unit, each with four 120hp traction motors. Power-operated doors are fitted — the first large-scale departure from the hinged 'slam' type of door characteristic of all Southern electric stock hitherto.

London Midland Region

The LMR is the only other Region still operating third rail dc emus. There have been fewer rolling stock developments in this category since World War II than on the Southern, but the 1,200V Manchester-Bury stock was replaced by the two-car units of Class 504 in 1959 and the stately 'Oerlikon' units on the Euston-Watford and Broad Street-Richmond services by the three-car sets of Class 501 in 1957. The Class 501 formation is motorcoach-trailer-driving trailer with a four-motor traction equipment in the

Below: Class 430 unit No 3005 heads two Class 491 trailer units on a Weymouth-Waterloo train in Clapham cutting. Brian Morrison

Top: The Manchester-Glossop-Hadfield sets are the only surviving 1,500V dc passenger trains. A Class 506 three-car unit arrives at Godley Junction bound for Hadfield. G. Roose

Above: The LMR still has low-voltage third-rail for local trains at Euston and on the North London line. A Class 501 unit leaves Richmond with the 13.25 to Broad Street. Harry Tabeart

Below right: A new generation of emus began with Class 507 in 1978. Unit No 507.005 is at Ormskirk on a Merseyrail working to Liverpool. R. T. Foster

motorcoach, the motors in each bogie connected permanently in parallel.

In 1937 the LMS electrified its lines in the Wirral and introduced the present three-car units of Class 503. A year later the company began replacement of its Liverpool-Southport stock with the present Class 502 units. In both classes the four motors in each motorcoach are controlled as two individual pairs, as was the general practice at the time of their introduction. This rolling stock is being replaced by three-car Class 507 units, generally similar to the Southern's four-car Class 508s. The first 507s were commissioned in 1978 soon after completion of the Loop and Link lines of the Merseyrail system in Liverpool. The Loop is, in effect, a 'turning circle' by means of which trains entering Liverpool from the Wirral make a circuit under the city and return without reversal. There is interchange at Moorfields and Central stations with the Link, and at Lime Street with the LMR main line terminus above. The Link connects the Liverpool-Southport/Ormskirk section with an extension of third rail electrification to Garston over the former Cheshire Lines Committee line. The branch from Walton Junction on the Ormskirk line to Kirkby has also been electrified. Class 507 units provide a service of a kind becoming increasingly common in large conurbations on the Continent, providing through running between areas previously served from separate termini, with underground stations in the city centre and easy interchange for journeys not covered by through trains.

Of the ac emus on the LMR, the four-car classes 304/1, 304/2 and 304/3 date from the early years of the 25kV electrification and were equipped originally with germanium rectifiers. All have now been replaced with silicon. It was decided from the outset that the traction equipment of all ac emus should be below floor level, and since the transformer, rectifier, and auxiliaries would occupy all available space under the motorcoach, the battery, charger and main compressor were moved to the adjacent driving trailer — known as a battery driving trailer. This arrangement has been used on all ac emus on the LM, Eastern and Scottish Regions up to and including Class 312.

When the LMR electrification reached London, more emus were needed for outer-suburban and semi-fast services. By that time the silicon rectifier was well established and in the Class 310 units of 1966 a rectifier of that type was used with natural cooling by the air flow under the train, the same flow cooling the transformer oil so that the radiator and motor-driven fan of earlier units were eliminated. The diodes were insulated electrically from the main heat sinks by discs of beryllium oxide, this material being a good conductor of heat as well as an electrical insulator. Class 310 was the first of the ac emus with disc brakes. In 1976 the LMR received four Class 312 units for operating West Midlands PTE services. This class is a development of Class 310 and is built in three versions for Eastern and LM Region duties. Progress in semi-

Below: A Class 310 unit forms a Euston-Rugby stopping service, seen at Northchurch. Alan N. Pierce

Right: Two Eastern Region Class 312s emerge from Wood Green Tunnel on a Royston-Kings Cross service. Les Bertram

Below right: Class 313 dual-voltage unit No 313.002 approaches Ponsbourne Tunnel on the Hertford North branch. Martin Higginson

conductors over the decade since Class 310 was introduced enabled the number of diodes in the rectifier to be reduced from 48 to 16.

The LMR operates the only remaining 1,500V dc passenger service on BR with the eight three-car sets of Class 506 running between Manchester Piccadilly, Glossop and Hadfield. These units were ordered in 1939 but work on them did not begin until after the war. Seating throughout the motorcoach-trailer-driving trailer unit is in open saloons with air-operated sliding doors.

Above: The Clacton emus on the Eastern Region, designed for 90mph maximum, were classified as 'high speed' in their day. Class 309/3 four-car unit leads a Clacton train through Colchester, passing an unusual visitor in the shape of No 40.186. John Chalcraft

Eastern Region

Early ac emus in the Eastern Region began life with mercury-arc rectifiers, but germanium diodes were used in converting ex-1500V dc stock for the new system. Many germanium rectifiers have since been replaced by silicon. Conversion of all Class 307 and some of Class 306 has been carried out in stages, with different arrangements, over the years. The last of the Class 305/2 units was fitted with a silicon rectifier and the experience gained with it encouraged the adoption of silicon for the 'Clacton Electrics' of Class 309 in its four varieties. With their balancing speed of 90mile/h in weak field the Class 309 units were regarded as 'high-speed' in their day and considered as probable forerunners of a fleet of express emus for other routes with heavier ruling grades. In the dc/ac conversions of Classes 306 and 307 mentioned above, the rectifier and transformer were mounted under the vehicle next to the motorcoach, which retained its dc control equipment — an arrangement foreshadowing the Class 313 units of 1976.

Class 313 was the first BR motive power equipped for operation on 25kV ac and 750V dc, this being necessary for the Hertford/Welwyn-Moorgate services of the GN suburban electrification. They were also the first BR emus, other than prototypes, with rheostatic braking and waste heat recovery from the resistances for carriage heating. The resistors are permanently cooled by a motor-driven fan, which is speeded up when they are in circuit for acceleration or braking. The Westcode air braking system is described in Section 8. Units are coupled by Tightlock automatic couplers on the outer vehicles, operated electrically from a driving compartment. The couplers contain all the mechanical, pneumatic and electrical connections necessary for operation of units in multiple.

The first 312 units in traffic were Class 312/2 on the LMR, but most of the class were for the Kings Cross-Hitchin-Royston service (312/0) and the GE Section (312/1), the latter having 25/6.25kV changeover equipment for services to and from Liverpool Street. The 312/1s were the first to be delivered. Replacement of the ex-dc Class 306 with new Class 315 thyristor-controlled four-car units was due to begin in 1980. These units and a similar three-car version for Scotland, Class 314, are the first BR production series of emus with thyristor control, implementing the decision taken in 1975 to adopt this system instead of tap-changer control for future construction.

Scottish Region

Electrification in Scotland began with the Airdrie-Helensburgh line and branches in 1960, for which the three-car units of Class 303 were built. These were equipped originally with mercury-arc rectifiers but later converted to silicon. As electrification continued south of the Clyde, more generally similar units were built, forming Class 311, equipped with silicon rectifiers from the outset and with the motor rating raised from 207 to 220hp. In this class the transformer oil was pumped through the rectifier cubicles to cool the diodes, heat being removed from the oil as it passed through a tank in which there were a number of tubes of about $2\frac{1}{2}$in dia through which airflow was maintained by the movement of the train. The electrified lines north and south of the Clyde in Glasgow were linked by the new Argyle Line and deliveries of the Class 314 units mentioned above coincided with the introduction of new Clyderail services over this connection.

8 The Air Brake

As originally planned, the Westinghouse air brake was not fail-safe. Its advantage in its early days was that it was a continuous brake acting on all the vehicles of a train under the control of the driver. The brake cylinders on each vehicle were connected to a brakepipe to which air under pressure could be admitted from a reservoir on the locomotive. Flexible hoses provided the connection between the brakepipes on individual vehicles so that effectively there was a continuous pipe throughout the train. When air was admitted to the pipe it entered the cylinders and forced the pistons out, so that through a system of cranks and levers the brake blocks were pressed against the wheels. The braking force could be controlled by stopping the flow of air into the cylinders, but the brakes could not be partially released after they had been applied. Release was obtained by opening the brakepipe to the atmosphere, which exhausted the air in the cylinders and caused the brake blocks to be fully withdrawn from the wheels.

With the above system a burst hose could cause a brake failure and the driver would not be aware of it until he tried to make an application, but with duplicate brakepipes and other precautions it was found acceptable for some time. It is usually called the 'straight' air brake, and although no longer used as a continuous system it is still fitted to locomotives for braking when running light. When the locomotive is coupled to a train the action of the 'straight' brake is coordinated with that of the continuous brake on the vehicles and operated by the same control.

The air brake was later made fail-safe by 'inverting' its method of operation, ie by making a *fall* in brakepipe pressure apply the brakes. This is the 'automatic' air brake as used for continuous braking today.

In its basic form the automatic brake applies the brakes throughout a train by allowing air stored under pressure in a reservoir on every vehicle to enter the brake cylinders. The reservoirs are connected to a brakepipe running the length of the train as already described. In normal running the brakepipe and reservoir pressures are the same. To apply the brakes, pressure in the brakepipe is reduced and the pressure difference causes a valve to connect the reservoirs to the brake cylinders.

The force with which the brake blocks are applied to the wheels depends on how far the brakepipe pressure has been reduced by the driver in moving his air brake control. The brakes are released by venting air direct to atmosphere, and in the basic system as in the 'straight' brake release has to be complete. Pressure in the reservoirs falls as air enters the brake cylinders, and when it is equal to that in the brakepipe the valve cuts off the supply of further air to the cylinders.

Originally the valve which connected the brakepipe to the reservoirs, or the reservoirs to the cylinders, or vented the cylinders to atmosphere, was called a 'triple valve'. Today the corresponding device is called a 'distributor' and it differs from the triple valve in the important respect that it allows the release of the brakes as well as a brake application to be graduated. BR has adopted a two-pipe system which is a variant of the one described, designed to speed up brake release. Here the brakepipe serves only for the control of braking, the reservoirs being kept charged from a second pipe — the main reservoir pipe. The auxiliary reservoirs on the vehicles are connected to the main reservoir pipe through a one-way valve as shown in Fig 20. If there is a loss of pressure in this pipe the air in

Fig 20 The two-pipe air brake system standardised by BR

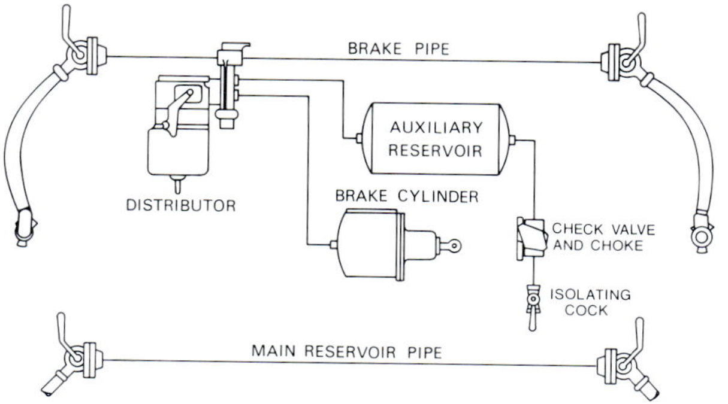

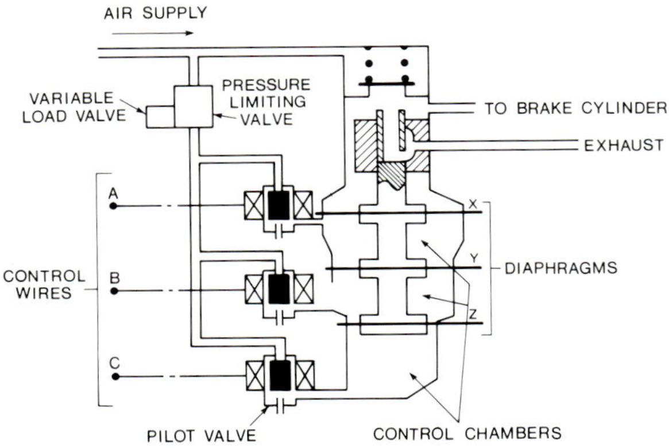

Fig 21 Westcode electropneumatic brake controller

the reservoirs is still held and when the driver makes a brake application the system reverts to single-pipe working.

With a distributor allowing graduated release of brakes as in this system, the brakes can only be released to the same extent as pressure in the brakepipe is restored. Shortening of the time necessary to recharge the pipe therefore speeds up release, and in the two-pipe system the brake valve on the locomotive has only to supply sufficient air to recharge the brakepipe itself and is not required to recharge the auxiliary reservoirs.

When air is used both as the control and the operating medium, the brakes are not applied or released simultaneously throughout a train because of the time it takes for a change in pressure to travel through the pipe from end to end of the train. Many improvements have been made in the system and the delay is negligible for most purposes, but simultaneous action is an advantage for services with short station stops and quick turn-rounds. To meet this requirement the electropneumatic brake was developed, in the first place particularly for emu stock. In this system the brakes are applied by venting air from the brakepipe through an electrically-operated valve on each vehicle, thus reducing the brakepipe pressure and causing the distributor to admit air to the brake cylinders. Similar valves exhaust air from the cylinders via the distributor exhausts to release the brakes. The ep system is an adjunct to the ordinary two-pipe air brake and does not affect its basic mode of operation. Both systems are controlled by the same brake handle so that if the electric valves fail to operate when an application is called for, the brakes are applied in the normal way by the fall in brakepipe pressure.

Recent developments in ep braking have extended the scope of electric control. In the latest emu classes electrical signals from the brake controller are transmitted through the unit and vary the output pressure from a relay valve in each vehicle which supplies air to the brake cylinders. The relay valve is shown in Fig. 21. Control wires A, B, C running through the train control three pilot valves in each relay. When a wire is de-energised its pilot valve opens, and by opening them in various combinations the pressure applied to the brake cylinders can be varied in up to seven steps. Three diaphragms, X, Y, Z, of different sizes, are connected to the stem of the main valve. Assuming pilot valve A to be de-energised, it opens and allows air from the supply to pass into the chamber below diaphragm X. The force on the diaphragm lifts the valve stem upwards, opening the inlet valve and allowing air to pass into the brake cylinder. When the pressure in the cylinder, acting on the upper side of the diaphragm, balances the upward force the inlet valve is closed by its spring. This gives one step of brake cylinder pressure. Further steps are obtained by opening the other valves in turn and in combination. The sizes of the diaphragms are proportioned so that each lifts the inlet valve with a greater force, so that a higher pressure is built up in the brake cylinder before it recloses.

The variable load valve enables the supply pressure to the diaphragm chambers to be varied according to the load of the individual coach so that the seven steps of braking are also modified to suit the load and the retardation throughout the train is uniform. The variable load valve can be operated by air pressure from the suspension of air-sprung vehicles, or by a signal derived from the deflection of mechanical springs.

When a train has both electropneumatic and rheostatic braking, both are controlled by the same handle. Provided the rheostatic system builds up correctly, the ep brake is held in reserve until rheostatic braking fades with falling speed. The ep brake then comes into action automatically to bring the train to a standstill, and it will also do so if there is a fault during the rheostatic period. In practice a small air pressure is maintained in the brake cylinders while the rheostatic brake is functioning so that the brake shoes are held in contact with the discs, but not exerting pressure on them. Therefore when the time comes for the ep brake to take over the shoes are in position to take effect at once.

The seven-step system described is the Westcode system. Others have similar characteristics and all in use by BR are compatible.

9 125mile/h and Above

by Roger Ford

British Rail has a dual strategy for providing high speed (over 100mile/h) passenger services. The High Speed Train, which entered service in October 1976, is based on the further development of conventional railway engineering, while the Advanced Passenger Train, undergoing running trials in 1980 represents a completely new technology in many respects. The most significant feature of both trains is that they are designed to provide high speed services on existing lines. This is in contrast with overseas railways, notably the Japanese and French, where intensive high speed operation depends on the construction of new lines — such as the Japanese Shinkansen.

Chronologically the Advanced Passenger Train (APT) came first. Fundamental research work at the Railway Technical Centre, Derby, in the early 1960s, on the riding of freight vehicles, resulted in a working theory of vehicle dynamics which assured a safe ride for the steel wheel on steel rail at speeds of 150mile/h and above. From this stemmed the concept of a passenger train able to run at 155mile/h on existing tracks, making the maximum use of BR's existing infrastructure. The APT project was unveiled in 1967. Meeting the specification involved major advances in three areas.

The first problem to be overcome was the effect of track curvature. When a train rounds a curve at speed, centrifugal force pushes the passengers sideways. This lateral acceleration can be reduced by canting or 'banking' the track. The remaining lateral acceleration is called cant deficiency and on BR this is limited to the equivalent of 4.5° of cant. It should be noted that speed restrictions on curves are purely for passenger comfort; the cant deficiency needed to overturn a train being in the region of 25°. The maximum cant used by BR is 6° and the minimum radius curve with this cant which a conventional train can negotiate at 125mile/h, within the passenger comfort limit of 4.5° of cant deficiency, is 5,900ft. The restriction this imposes can be judged from the fact that, of BR's major trunk routes, approximately 50% of the mileage is made up of curves and about 50% of these curves are relatively sharp with radii between 1,760ft and 6,600ft. APT overcomes the limitation on cant deficiency by tilting through curves. By tilting the APT vehicles inward by 9° the train can negotiate curves at speeds equivalent to a 9° cant deficiency while the passengers experience no lateral

acceleration whatsoever. The effect of this tilting is to raise the speed through curves by between 20% and 40%.

Running up to 50% faster than conventional trains on existing track led to the second major innovation. The limitation on speed in these circumstances is not installed horsepower but the ability to stop within existing signalling distances. In the case of APT the necessary stopping power is provided by hydrokinetic or 'water turbine' brakes. On the APT passenger vehicles the hydrokinetic brakes are mounted within the large-diameter hollow axles. When the brake is filled with fluid (a water/glycol mixture) it develops a retarding torque. The energy of braking is converted into heat as angular momentum is created and destroyed within the fluid. Brake force is controlled by varying the pressure in the system. The brake itself circulates the fluid to a reservoir mounted in the vehicle. Because the hydrokinetic brake loses its effectiveness at low speeds conventional tread friction braking is fitted and is progressively blended in below 50mile/h.

The third outstanding feature of APT is its combination of low weight and low aerodynamic drag which result in high energy efficiency. Low weight starts with aluminium construction of the passenger vehicles. In the three prototype (APT-P) trains, the construction is based on wide aluminium extrusions which run the full length of the vehicle and are welded together along the seams. This form of construction gives a 40% weight saving over conventional steel construction. Further weight saving results from the adoption of articulation which reduces the number of bogies for a train. The passenger vehicles are 2m shorter than the standard BR Mk II coach but provide the same number of seats. This is achieved by having only one door per side and locating the toilet in the vestibule space. The toilets themselves are of the recirculating chemical type and save $\frac{3}{4}$ton per coach.

Top left: Power car of the prototype APT (APT-P). This is a non-driving vehicle but driving power cars will be built for the production trains. BR

Left: Driving car and two passenger saloons of the APT-P. BR

Because of clearances needed when tilted, the APT vehicles have a smaller cross section than conventional passenger vehicles. Together with the streamlined nose and tail and overall surface smoothness this means that an 11-coach APT will have only 61% of the aerodynamic drag and 68% of the total train resistance of an electrically-hauled train of Mk III coaches with the same passenger capacity.

The three prototype trains are propelled by separate power cars with a rating of 4,000hp. The 25kV ac electrical equipment is thyristor controlled with separately-excited traction motors. The traction motors are mounted inside the body and drive the axles through cardan shafts. The trains can be marshalled as one power car plus 11 trailer vehicles for 125mile/h operation or two + 12 for 150mile/h running. The power cars are marshalled in the centre of the formation. This is because it was thought that it would not be possible to build a driving power car, with the additional weight of cab and buffing gear, within the axle load specified by the civil engineers. However, the APT-P power cars have turned out lighter than forecast and production trains will have a driving power car at one end in a one + 10 formation.

Little has been required to adapt the existing railway to APT use. While the trains will be able to operate at 125mile/h within the existing signalling, they will have higher speeds through curves than the restrictions indicated at the trackside for conventional trains which will be running at the same time as APT. Instead of having separate trackside indications at the approach to curves, showing the speeds for both conventional trains and APT, the APT driver receives a visual indication of the permitted speed in the cab. This is provided by a transponder on the track at the approach to each speed restriction. A receiver mounted underneath the APT interrogates the transponder which contains a permanently encoded signal giving the appropriate speed restriction. This signal is decoded on board the APT and displayed digitally in a panel in front of the driver. The display gives the permitted speed at all times, thus, after the train has passed through a curve and is on straight track, the display will return to 125. If the restriction is due to a junction, the speed indication includes the suffix J.

The APT-P and the first series production trains will run on the West Coast main line. When the overhead line equipment for this route was installed it was designed for a maximum speed of

Above: HST No 254.012 passes Doncaster with an afternoon Newcastle-Kings Cross service. I. J. Hodson

100mile/h. However, it has proved suitable for 125mile/h operation, at least, with only minor changes, essentially, an increase in contact wire tension and the maintenance of this tension within closer limits. The APT-P uses a new design of pantograph with a three stage suspension. The pantograph is supported on a frame linked to the power car bogie which ensures that the pantograph does not tilt with the train but is fully suspended.

The APT development programme was authorised in 1969. By 1973 development work, including running with the gas-turbine powered APT-E, had proved the concept and in 1974, the construction of the APT-P trains was authorised with the ultimate aim of squadron APT service in 1982. However, by 1970 it had become clear that the commercial need for higher speed and improved comfort on BR could not wait while new technology was developed. Thus in August 1970 the BR Chief Mechanical & Electrical Engineer's Department was authorised to build a diesel powered High Speed Train (HST) to improve journey times on major non electrified routes where competition from motorways and air traffic was making inroads on the railways' passenger business. The prototype train was completed in 22 months, although testing was then held up for nine months due to Union 'blacking' of the cab arrangement of the APT and HST with central driver's seat.

The HST represents the conventional railway engineering approach to 125mile/h running. Passenger accommodation is provided by a rake of seven to nine British Rail Mk III coaches. These are of conventional steel construction, are fully air-conditioned, have air bag secondary suspension, and all axles are disc braked. The main technical challenge was providing the 4,500hp needed to propel the train at 125mile/h within the axle load limit. The standards for acceptable track stresses are those imposed by a Class 55 locomotive at 100mile/h. Track stresses depend both on axle load and un-sprung mass. Thus the Class 55 locomotive has an unsprung mass of $3\frac{1}{4}$ tons per axle, the HST, for 125mile/h running, 2.16 tons while the APT-P (designed for 150mile/h) has an unsprung mass of 1.375 tons. On the HST, this is achieved by mounting the traction motors on the bogie frame instead of on the axles, as in conventional diesel locomotives. The axle load was also limited to 17.5 tons. To provide the required power within these constraints two power cars were necessary together with a highly rated diesel engine. The engine selected was the Paxman Valenta giving 2,250hp at 1,500rev/min. Each engine drives an alternator, the current from which is rectified to feed direct current traction motors. Apart from the use of electronic control equipment, the traction equipment is conventional. The Mk III coaches are also identical to those used for 100mile/h locomotive hauled services on the West Coast main line except that ac power for air conditioning and catering vehicles, lighting, etc, is supplied from the alternator in one power car rather than through a motor alternator set on each coach.

As with APT, the main feature of the HST is its ability to run at 125mile/h within signal spacings designed for 100mile/h. In other words, the train can stop from 125mile/h in the same distance required to stop a 100mile/h conventional express. This is achieved through the disc brakes on the train. These have turned out to be the most highly stressed part of the HST, leading to problems with discs fracturing due to the thermal effects of heavy braking.

Only one special concession has been required for 125mile/h HST running. This concerns signalling arrangements at the approach to diverging junctions where a speed restriction applies to one arm of the junction only. A driver approaching the junction in a conventional train can safely pass the signal before the junction at a speed which will enable him to stop in time if the signal after the junction showed a red aspect. With HST, because of the improved braking performance, the speed past the signal before the junction could be higher than that of a conventional train in the same situation. While both trains could stop at the next signal, the HST could, if the driver saw the junction indicator at the last moment, pass through the facing points of the junction at too high a speed. To avoid this possibility, while not unduly restricting speed through the junction, a new flashing yellow aspect has been introduced to alert HST drivers approaching a junction with a less than line speed divergence.

While both APT and HST run on 'existing track', routes scheduled for 125mile/h operation are prepared to higher standards of top and line (vertical and lateral alignment) and have a greater depth of ballast. Running experience on the Western Region to date has shown that the effect on lateral alignment of high speed running has been less than expected. Vertical alignment has suffered more than expected but contributory factors to this include frequent fast, heavy freight trains over the route. Track condition is checked by the High Speed Recording coach which can be marshalled in an HST and will measure and record track irregularities with great accuracy at 125mile/h. To maximise the investment in the 125mile/h capability of HST, routes on which the train will operate have speed restrictions eased where possible. This can take the form of slewing the track to straighten out a curve. The cant can also be increased up to a maximum of 6in (6°).

Special maintenance facilities have been provided for HST and are in course of provision for APT. Each HST returns to its depot for maintenance every other day. To maximise utilisation, maintenance is carried out overnight. The train is maintained as a fixed formation — although failed vehicles are 'cut-out' and replaced — and the roads in the depot are designed with special facilities for the power car at each end.

10 Signalling

Despite the very different appearance of semaphore and colour-light signalling, both are founded on the 'absolute block' principle. This implies that the line is divided by the signals into block sections, and that only one train must be in a section at any given time. Usually this method of working is simply called the 'block system', but strictly speaking it is 'absolute block', to distinguish it from the 'permissive block' operated on some goods lines and in other special circumstances, for example when two passenger trains have to be accommodated at the same platform. Special rules apply in these situations, and before a train is admitted to an occupied section it is brought almost to a halt. Usually a small subsidiary signal rather than the main block signal is used to give permission to proceed.

In semaphore signalling the passage of trains from one block section to the next is controlled by a sequence of signals, of which an example is shown in Fig 22. Signals with square-ended arms are 'stop' signals and must not be passed when in the horizontal 'danger' position. Those with a notched end to the arm are 'distant' signals. When horizontal their message is 'caution' and the driver must be prepared to stop at a stop signal ahead. This may not necessarily be the next one he comes to. In the diagram Parkhurst distant would be at 'caution' ('on') if the Parkhurst starter was at 'danger' (also called 'on'), but the outer home and inner home signals would be showing 'clear' ('off'). At one time signal arms

Fig 22 Semaphore signalling block section

THE BLOCK SYSTEM

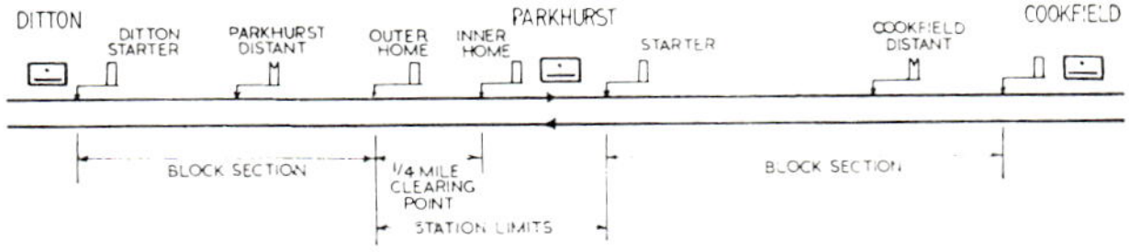

were generally lowered to show 'off' but today they are raised into the upper quadrant, except for a few survivors of the older type.

Referring again to the diagram, the $\frac{1}{4}$-mile clearing point between Parkhurst outer and inner home signals will be noted. Usually this has to be clear as well as the block section itself between Ditton starter and Parkhurst outer home before the signalman at Ditton can pull his starter 'off' to let a train enter the section.

This basic example shows a stretch of plain track with no diverging lines or crossings. In semaphore signalling signals at junctions have separate arms for the different routes, the arm for the direction straight ahead being on the main post and higher than those for diverging routes, which are mounted on short posts supported from the main post on a bracket.

Communication between signalboxes in mechanically signalled areas is by means of electric block instruments, using a code of special bell signals. For a detailed account of signalling today, both mechanical and colour-light, readers are referred to *British Railway Signalling* by G. M. Kichenside and Alan Williams (Ian Allan Ltd, fourth edition 1978).

In mechanically signalled areas the line is regarded as normally blocked, and is only opened for the passage of a train when required. This practice is known as 'closed block' working. In the early days of the block system some railways favoured the 'open block', and signals were normally 'off', but set at 'on' behind a train to protect it when it entered a section. The Great Northern Railway operated an 'open block' until after the Abbots Ripton accident of 1876. The double collision on that occasion followed failure of a signal to go to 'danger' because the slot in the post inside which the arm was pivoted was clogged with snow. Failure to go to 'clear' would obviously have less dangerous consequences, and the Inspecting Officer who inquired into the accident recommended that the closed block principle should be applied to all passenger lines.

Today some 40% of British Railways is signalled with colour-lights, usually working automatically except in station and junction areas, and the open block has returned. The automatic colour-light signal shows a green light continuously while the section between it and the next signal ahead, plus an 'overlap' corresponding to the clearing point mentioned earlier, is unoccupied. But the block principle is observed as strictly as before, the block section now extending from one signal to the next.

Four standard aspects are used in BR colour-light signalling:

	Colour	*Meaning*
1	Red	Stop
2	Single Yellow	Prepare to stop at next signal
3	Double Yellow	Advance caution warning. Next signal at single yellow
4	Green	Line clear

Below: Colour-light signal with four-light directional route indicators (top) and below the main four-aspect signal head, a position-light subsidiary signal with stencil route indicator. GEC-General Signal

These aspects were recommended by a committee of the Institution of Railway Signal Engineers which reported in 1924. It was known at first as the 'Three-position signal committee', the original intention being to legislate for semaphore signals, but it soon became apparent that the colour-light was the signal of the future and so the name was changed to 'Three-aspect committee'. At this period the South Eastern & Chatham suburban lines of the Southern Railway were being electrified. Here steam-hauled expresses running at up to 80mile/h and electric multiple-units with a top speed of about 55mile/h, and more effective braking, would share the same tracks in some places. The signal spacing sufficient for an emu sighting a yellow to stop at the following red signal was too short for an express, which needed earlier warning. A wider spacing of signals would reduce the line capacity, and so the committee recommended a fourth aspect — double-yellow — to precede the single-yellow. Thus the familiar four-aspect signalling came into being and has proved adequate for the highest speeds up to the present time. A fifth aspect — flashing yellow — for the special case of High Speed Trains approaching diverging junctions has been approved by the Railway Inspectorate (see Section 9).

Multiple-aspect signalling is usually denoted by the contraction 'mas'. By its nature every signal in an mas scheme can act as a home or a distant or an 'outer distant' signal. A bracket construction with separate signal heads for main and diverging routes can be seen at some junctions but current practice is to use a single signal head with a route indicator. This is an inclined row of white lights which are illuminated only when a diverging route has to be taken. Where there is one diverging route the indicator is inclined at 45°; if there are two there is a second indicator at 90°, and if three a third at 135°. According to the direction of divergence, the indicators point to left or right of the signal post. Thus, with one route turning left and the other right, there would be two indicators at 45°, one pointing in each direction.

Junction signals are usually preceded by an ordinary signal with a single head which shows a yellow aspect when a diverging route has to be taken. The junction signal may be held at red until the train is approaching it, ensuring that the turn-out is taken at low-speed. As the driver draws near he sees the signal change to green and the route indicator light up, and he applies power again. At some junctions this procedure would slow the movement of trains

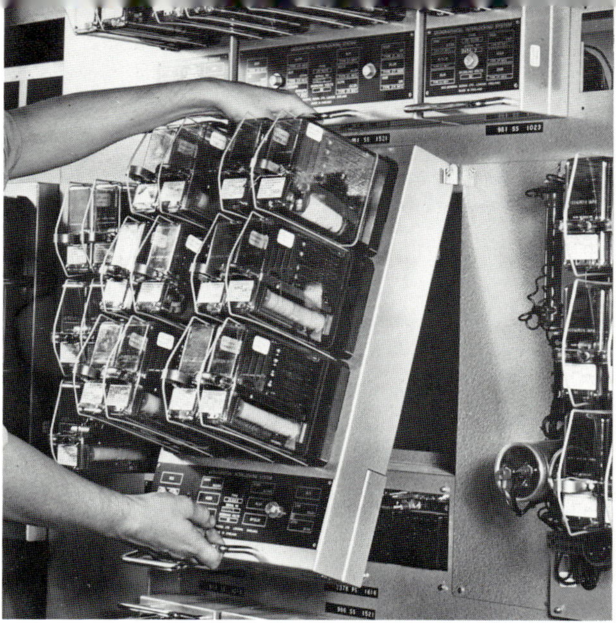

Above: A pre-wired jack-in set of miniature plug-in relays as used in 'geographical' interlockings. GEC-General Signal

more than is necessary. When a diverging route is set up, therefore, the junction signal goes to yellow, with its route indicator illuminated, and the preceding signal shows double-yellow.

The operation of colour-light signals depends on track circuits. Even when a signal is being controlled by a signalman, it will be restored automatically to red behind a train by track circuit action. Fundamentally, a track circuit consists of a length of track electrically insulated from the adjacent sections at each end of it. A low-voltage source is connected across the rails at one end — the 'feed' end — and an electrical relay at the other. When no train is present, current flows from the source along one rail, through the relay coil, and back to the source through the other rail. In these conditions the relay is energised and a pivoted armature is attracted towards the electromagnet formed by the coil and its iron core. When a train is in the track circuit, however, its wheels and axles provide a path for the current of lower resistance than the coil, the coil is short-circuited and the armature is released. In moving to and fro the armature operates contacts controlling many external functions.

Track circuits may be fed with direct or alternating current, the latter being used on lines electrified for dc traction. Here there must be provision for one or both rails to carry return traction current. If only one is required for this purpose, the insulated rail joints which separate the track circuits are fitted in the other rail only. If both rails are used for traction return, insulated joints are fitted in both rails but they are by-passed by impedance bonds which allow the traction current to flow but block the track circuit current. An impedance bond consists of a pair of iron-cored coils connected across the rails so that one coil is on each side of the insulated joints. The coils obstruct the passage of ac but offer no appreciable resistance to dc, which flows past the joints through a connection between a centre tapping in each coil.

A signalling relay of the 'miniature' dc pattern now standardised by BR is shown in Fig 23. 'Miniature' is a relative term. The present relays perform the same number of functions as earlier

Fig 23   Miniature dc plug-in signalling relay

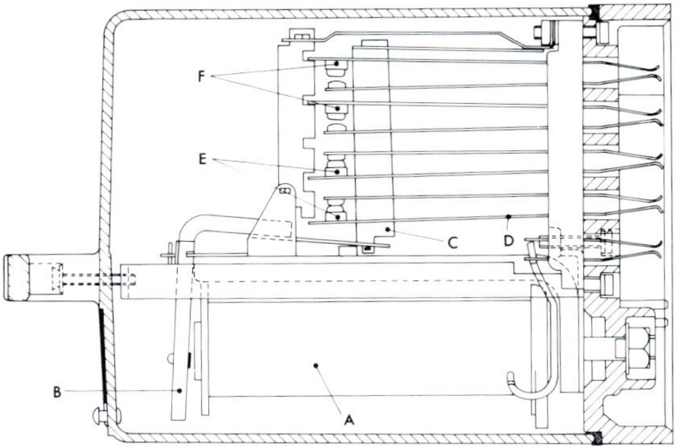

designs in about one-sixth or one-tenth the space, but much smaller relays are used in other forms of telecommunications and control engineering. Referring to the diagram, when the electromagnet A is energised, armature B is attracted towards it and lifts the insulated bar C, which engages with the strips of spring metal D carrying the contacts. In this example the normally closed lower pair of contacts E separate ('back' contacts) and the normally open upper ones, F, close ('front' contacts). When the relay is de-energised, eg by the presence of a train in a track circuit, the springs are no longer under compression and they return to the positions shown in the diagram, moving the armature away from the electromagnet in so doing.

Connections to the relay contacts are made automatically when relays of the type described are plugged into plugboards, the outer ends of the springs being shaped to form plug-in contacts. A coded pattern of registration pins on the relay corresponds with holes in the plugboard to ensure that a relay can only be plugged into the position appropriate to its function.

A circuit using track relays for automatic colour-light signalling is shown in simplified form in Fig 24. The points marked + in the diagram are connected to the signalling power supply and the three aspects of signal 1 are represented by the letters G, Y, and R. In the

Fig 24 Automatic control of colour-light signals

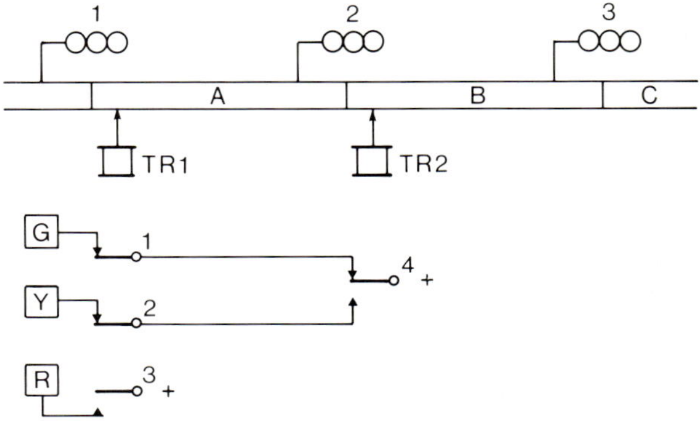

condition shown track circuits A, B, and C are all unoccupied. Signal 1 is showing green, its green aspect lamp being connected to the supply through front contacts in relays TR2 and TR1. Consider, now, a train passing signal 1 and entering track circuit A. TR1 will be de-energised and its contacts will drop. The feed to the green aspect will be broken by contact 1, and contact 3 (a back contact) will connect a feed to the red aspect.

When the train passes signal 2 and enters track circuit B, TR2 will be de-energised but TR1 will 'pick-up', ie its contacts will return to the conditions shown. Only the yellow aspect will be illuminated, however, because contact 4 of TR2 has dropped, breaking the feed to signal 1 green and making a feed via a back contact and TR1 contact 2 to signal 1 yellow. Signal 2 is showing red for reasons similar to those described in connection with signal 1.

Next the train enters track circuit C. Accordingly TR2 is energised again and its contact 4 restores the feed to signal 1 green, simultaneously breaking the feed to the yellow aspect. In practice G, Y and R would not be the signal lamps themselves but signal relays which, when energised, would 'switch on' the corresponding signal lamps by connecting them to a separate circuit, and this, in turn, would not be connected direct to the lamps but to one of the step-down transformers in the signal head.

In many relays for ac track circuits the contacts are operated by a moving vane which is driven by currents induced in it similarly to the vane which can be seen revolving inside an ordinary domestic electricity meter. Relays of this type normally work on a 50Hz supply. When a line is electrified for 50Hz traction, dc track circuits may be used if one rail is available for them, but if traction and signalling currents have to flow in both rails the ac for signalling must be of frequencies well removed from 50Hz to avoid interference. A high-frequency system now being widely applied uses electronic transmitters and receivers with vibrating reeds — similar to tuning forks — to stabilise the transmission frequency and to act as a filter at the receiver so that only the signalling frequency gets through to the output amplifier. The output is then rectified to operate a dc relay. This system can also be used instead of conventional 50Hz track circuits and moving vane ac relays on dc electrified lines.

The 'head' of a multi-unit colour-light signal contains the lenses and lamps for the two; three or four aspects it can display. Each aspect is a separate light-tight compartment in which the 110/24V transformer which feeds the lamp is also housed. The lamps usually operate at 24V and have two filaments, only one of which is in circuit at a time. If the filament in circuit fails, a relay operates which brings the second filament into circuit and at the same time transmits a warning to the box from which the signal is controlled.

In some situations it is difficult to install a conventional four-aspect signal head because of limited space. A 'searchlight' signal is then used, having only one lens and lamp, but an internal moving vane mechanism with coloured roundels to produce the red, yellow and green aspects. In four-aspect areas it is then necessary to add an extra unit with a lamp and yellow lens which is switched on to give the double-yellow aspect in conjunction with the yellow aspect of the searchlight itself.

Searchlight signals were once favoured in some quarters because it was impossible to produce a 'ghost' aspect by strong sunlight falling on a coloured lens — a condition most likely to arise on overseas railways. Current designs of lenses and lens hoods in multi-aspect signals have now made this risk negligible and the searchlight is confined to places where a space difficulty exists.

It will be noticed from Fig 24 that the track circuits do not coincide with the positions of the signals but that there is a short 'overlap'. This means that signal 2, for example, is held at red until a train is a certain distance past it. If track circuit A finished at the signal itself, signal 1 would go to yellow as soon as a train had passed the signal post. The overlap extends the zone of protection and ensures that if a driver overruns a signal at 'danger' he is still protected as long as he pulls up within the overlap. Sometimes overlaps extend from signal to signal (full block overlap). A train then always has two red signals behind it. Referring again to Fig 24, with a train in track circuit B signal 2 would show red, but signal 1 would show red as well because track circuit B is also the overlap of signal 2.

At one time electropneumatic operation of points predominated in power signalling installations, but with the extension of remote control of signalling over very long distances electric operation is now preferred. It is easier to provide an electric power supply for point machines at distant locations than to install compressors and air piping. An electric point machine converts the rotary drive of an electric motor into the push-pull action necessary to throw the

Above: Electric point machine with covers removed. The motor (nearest camera) drives the throw-bar (centre) through a triple-reduction gear train and clutch. GEC-General Signal

points. An electric motor drives a bevel gear through a speed-reducing gear train and clutch. The final gearwheel is mounted horizontally in the base of the machine. A roller-bearing 'crankpin' on its underside engages in a specially shaped aperture in the end of the throw bar so that as the wheel revolves the throwbar is moved forwards or backwards. At the end of the stroke the motor is either braked electrically or the clutch is disengaged automatically and the motor runs freely to rest. In either case, if the points meet an obstruction the clutch slips.

There is a further linkage from the final gearwheel to the locking slide which unlocks the points before the throw begins and locks them again in their new position. The points themselves are connected to detector slides in the machine which operate contacts involved in the control of the motor and the indication of the position of the points to the signalbox and the signalling circuits.

An alternative to electric operation of points is the electro-hydraulic clamp lock point machine developed by BR, first used on a wide scale in the London Bridge resignalling and installed throughout the layout at Cannon Street. Here the points are moved by hydraulic actuators supplied with oil under pressure from a power pack usually positioned at the side of the track adjacent to

Above: The control panel at Motherwell signalling centre.
GEC-General Signal

the points. A hook-shaped lock arm is pivoted from each switch rail (Fig 25) and passes under the stock rail as the switch rail moves towards it. It then lifts behind the stock rail to clamp the two rails firmly together. A coupling bar simultaneously unlocks and opens the other switch, its actuator retracting. Electric detection of the open or closed condition at each stock rail/switch rail is inherent in the action and controlled by cam-operated limit switches. In this machine the separate unlock/throw/lock operations of the conventional electric point machine are merged into one continuous action.

Signalling today is controlled on the route-setting principle. That is to say, instead of signals and points being controlled individually

Fig 25 BR electro-hydraulic point lock machine

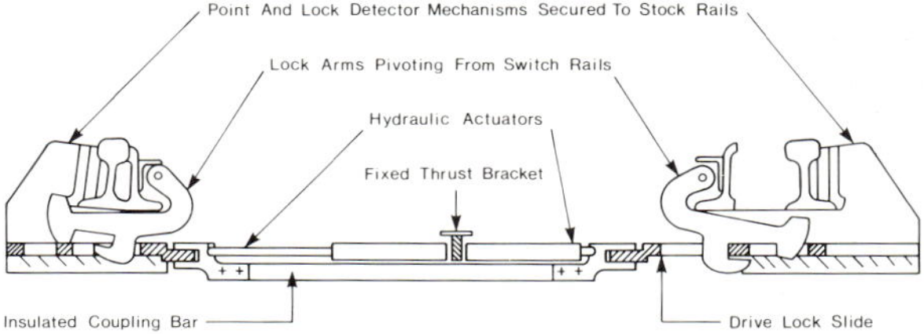

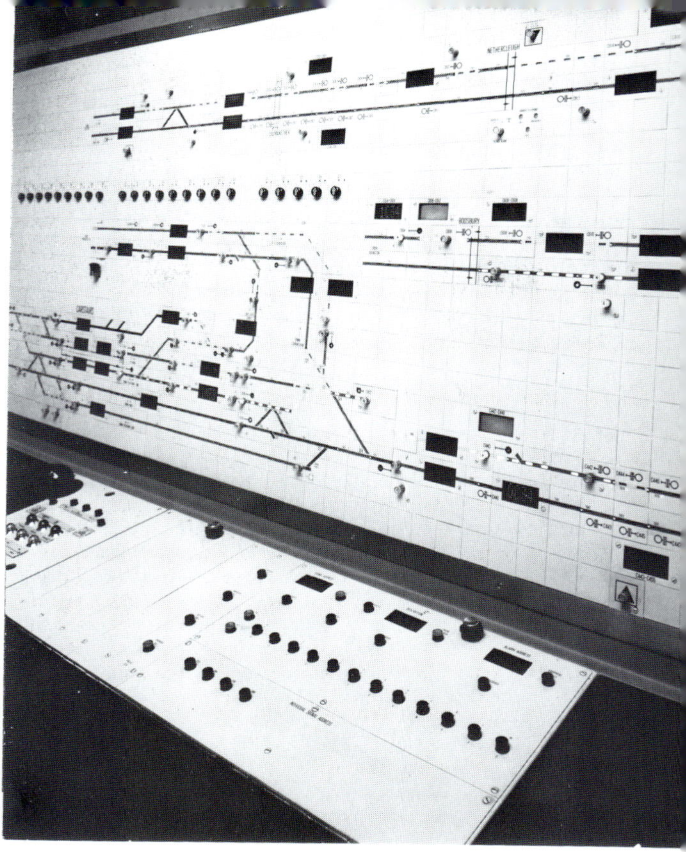

Above: Close-up of a section of the Motherwell panel showing control buttons and the train description apertures at signal berth positions on the diagram. GEC-General Signal

a simple pushbutton action sets the points and clear the signals for a complete route. In this context, a 'route' extends from one main running signal to the next, and it does not necessarily involve the operation of points. The preferred method of operation is by means of pushbuttons mounted on the track diagram in the signalbox. To set a route from signal A to signal B the signalman presses a button adjacent to the representation of each signal on the diagram. Assuming the train was to continue past B, the B pushbutton would be pressed a second time, followed by the button for signal C, and so on. This procedure is called 'entry/exit' control. In older installations the buttons had to be pulled to cancel a route before it could be set up again but it is becoming the practice to reset automatically from the track circuits.

Relay interlocking is a necessary accompaniment of panel control. Electric interlocking had been introduced before the first panels appeared in the 1930s but it acted on the small levers in the power frames of the period, locking them physically. Panel switches are always free to move, but if operated incorrectly the electric circuits do not respond. Here again a relay is an essential element. Fig 26 shows a simple case of interlocking between a signal and a pair of points. The relays are 'latching' relays, ie the contacts remain in the position to which they have been moved although the coil is de-energised. The relay coils are cross-connected. Thus, coil N of the signal relay, for example, closes contacts 1 and 2, and they remain closed when current through the coil is cut off. When coil R is energised, however, current flows through N in the opposite direction and releases the latch.

In the diagram, points relay coil N has been energised to set the points for the through route at a junction, and signal relay coil N is energised to clear the corresponding signal. To set the diverging route button A would be turned. Signal relay coil N would then be de-energised, but contacts 1 and 2 of the relay would remain closed because of the latch. This makes a feed from the lower segment of the A button via contact 1 to the R coil of the points relay, causing the points to be thrown for the diverging route. Energising R closes contact 3 and connects a feed via that contact and the upper A button segment to signal relay coil R, clearing the signal for the route. It also has the effect of unlatching contacts 1 and 2. Switch B is now isolated. The effect is similar to the locking of a main line signal lever when the points are set for the branch, except that in this case B is still free to move, although ineffective.

It is now the practice to group plug-in relays in sets on pre-wired panels, each set providing for a particular function such as the

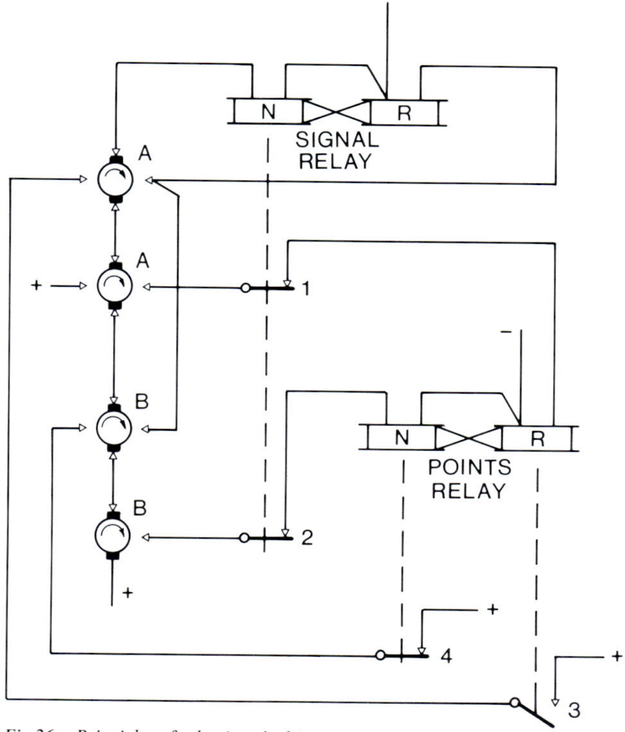

Fig 26 Principles of relay interlocking

control of a set of points and the associated signals. In the relay room the sets are arranged in a sequence corresponding to the geography of the track layout. This system is called 'geographical circuitry'. Complete sets can be removed from the racks and replaced as required and a system of coded pegs and holes ensures that a set can only be put back in the correct position. Individual relays can also be removed from the sets and, as explained earlier, are similarly coded to ensure correct replacement.

In past years experimental interlockings using solid-state logic devices instead of electromechanical relays were put in at Henley-on-Thames, WR, and Norton Bridge, LMR, but both have since been removed. Eventually, however, the relay is likely to be superseded. BR Research at Derby is working on a programme of solid state interlocking of which the first results are expected to be seen in 1981.

The major developments in BR signalling in recent years have been in the concentration of control and the development of the computer-based train describer. The operation of signalling over large areas from one panel is economic if a large number of remote interlockings can be controlled over one pair of wires. One method of doing this is to allot every item a brief 'time slot' in a continuously repeated cycle. Each time its slot comes round it is connected to the main highway to the control centre and in this fleeting period any necessary control signal is sent, and indications are received showing signal aspects, point settings and track circuit information for display on the control panel. Such a system is known as 'time division multiplex' (tdm). The control can be regarded as a signalman's 'long arm' reaching out to the distant interlockings and operating them in the same way as if they were close to the box, with every item connected to the control centre by its own pair of wires. At each remote site the instructions from control are carried out by local relays with the usual interlocking and other safeguards.

As well as concentrations of signalling at major interlockings, other functions have to be carried out at intermediate points. This can be achieved by connecting the equipment involved to a common two-wire circuit which carries up to some 80 control and indication channels on different frequencies, all of which can work simultaneously. This is known as 'frequency division multiplex' (fdm) and it depends on very accurate tuning of the transmitters and receivers so that equipment only responds to its allotted frequency. The tuned reed system already mentioned in connection with track circuits was developed originally for fdm control and is widely used in this application. In a large signalling scheme tdm and fdm systems often work side by side, the fdm system passing information to local relay rooms where it is incorporated with the main flow in the fdm system.

The types of train describers used for many years showed the signalman the class and destination of approaching trains. His track diagram showed him when track circuits became occupied and he used his own 'mental logic' to identify the trains concerned. An electronic train description system as used on signalling panels today positively identifies all trains on the board by displaying their individual descriptions as shown in the working timetable. The displays, presented on small cathode ray tubes visible through apertures in the panel, are adjacent to the positions of main running signals on the diagram and they show the identity of the train approaching such a signal at any time.

Descriptions are entered into the system by the signalmen operating buttons or switches on a set-up panel, but this is only necessary at the start of the journey, the descriptions being passed automatically from box to box thereafter. As the train moves through the area controlled by the box its description is stepped from signal to signal. The system therefore needs to be informed as successive track circuits are occupied, and to know how points are set. For example, if two trains are approaching a converging junction and the main line train is held at the junction signal, the description of the train coming from the branch will have to be stepped forward when the next track circuit on the main line is occupied. Simple deductions of this kind do not need a computer. They can be made by ordinary relay logic circuits, and this method was used at first, but it was soon found convenient to use a computer because if the 'logic' is written in the form of a computer program it can be modified to meet changing circumstances simply by changing the program. In the older method the whole system would have to be rewired.

Stepping descriptions alone would leave the computer with much unoccupied time and many other tasks have been found for it. Indeed, 'train describer' has become something of a misnomer and it would be more appropriate to speak of a computer-based train describer as a 'traffic information system'. Typical offshoots of the basic describer function are printout of train reports for management use, provision of train running information on demand for inquiry offices, etc, the control of platform indicators and recorded announcements, and operation of visual display units (vdus) showing the traffic situation in selected areas for the information of senior regulators, terminal station staff, and traffic managers. The working timetable can be held in the computer and the actual running of trains compared with it, discrepancies in time or route being printed out. This is called 'automatic train reporting by exception' (atre) and ensures that management is not flooded with computer print-out from which significant features have to be extracted by close scrutiny. Everything in the atre report is important.

With the timetable and train descriptions in the computer, automatic route-setting becomes a possibility and is being developed. Many other applications suggest themselves, but what is technically possible is not always economic and the latter criterion is strictly observed by BR.

The signalling practice described so far applies to double-track and multi-track main lines. For many years the working of single lines was based on the principle that a train entering a section between passing places must be in possession of a staff or token which was either unique in itself or, when issued from a machine, inhibited the issue of further tokens until it had been placed in a corresponding machine at the other end of the section. Today a system called 'tokenless block' is used on some lines. Under these rules a train can be admitted to a section when it has been proved clear by a preceding train occupying and clearing a track circuit on leaving the section in either direction, and the signalman at the exit end has assured himself that the train is complete by observing the tail lamp.

Two-way working over one track is not confined to single lines. Some tracks in busy mas areas near large stations are signalled for both directions to provide operational flexibility. Such sections are normally short, but in the course of preparations for 125mile/h services the Western Region installed reversible working throughout between Didcot and the approaches to Bristol via Chippenham and via Badminton. The object here was to reduce delays at weekends, when single-line working is often necessary to by-pass sections of track undergoing maintenance. Additional crossovers which trains could safely take at 40mile/h were installed at intervals between 6 and 10 miles so that they could switch from track to track. Special precautions were taken to safeguard men patrolling the track, who could cancel 'wrong-way' working by operating local switches after telephoning the signalman for his agreement.

Existing BR main line signalling is considered to be adequate for speeds up to 200km/h (125mile/h) and it is the driver's responsibility to observe and obey the signals at the lineside. The audible signals given in the cab by the automatic warning system (aws) are advisory only, although the brakes are applied automatically if they are ignored. This system was designed originally for speeds up to 140km/h (90mile/h) but performs reliably at 160km/h (100mile/h) and has since been further developed for operation at 200km/h. The aws installation on the track consists of a permanent magnet and an adjacent electromagnet, 200yd on the approach side of a signal. If the signal is clear, the electromagnet is energised and the trainborne magentic receiver detects the presence of two magnets, causing a bell to sound in the cab. If the signal is showing any aspect other than clear (eg double-yellow, yellow or red) the electromagnet is not energised and only the permanent magnet is detected by the train equipment. A horn in the cab sounds a warning, which the driver must acknowledge by pressing a pushbutton within 2 sec. If he fails to do so an automatic brake application is made. Acknowledging the warning silences the horn. The driver is reminded that he has acknowledged the warning and must prepare to reduce speed further or stop at a signal ahead by an indicator in the cab displaying alternate yellow and black segments. At the next signal the indicator is returned automatically to all-black.

The trainborne receiver contains a pivoted armature that is deflected by the permanent magnet every time it passes over a magnet site. This interrupts a circuit to a magnet valve in the braking system, but the valve is not released at once because of the energy stored in a capacitor, which is sufficient to hold it closed for one second. In that time the receiver will have reached the electromagnet, and if this is energised the armature will be deflected back to its original position, restoring the supply to the valve. If the electromagnet is not energised, however, the valve is released as soon as the condenser has discharged and braking takes place.

A system for advising APT drivers of speeds to observe has been installed on the Euston-Glasgow main line. The information is held in digital form in transponders mounted on the sleepers. When an APT passes over a transponder, it activates it by means of an electromagnetic field. There is sufficient energy in the field for the transponder to transmit the information it contains, which is displayed in the cab (see also Section 9).

Signalling in its many aspects today employs silicon devices over the whole range from individual transistors and diodes, through integrated circuits of varying complexity, up to microprocessors. The saving in space when the central processor of a computer can be formed on a single chip of silicon is particularly important when information transmitted to a train as in the case of the APT has to be processed on board. For maximum security, two computers are necessary and there would be problems in accommodating two of conventional form. For similar reasons the messages must be relatively long, containing elements for checking accuracy and rejecting any which have become mutilated in transmission, and the ability to handle messages of this type would increase the size of a conventional computer. In the APT installation, known as C-APT (Control — Advanced Passenger Train), two microprocessors in one computer decode each message independently; one of them displays the information to the driver and both together check that the display is correct. If either detects a fault it causes a fuse to blow which isolates that computer and switches in a standby.

Transponders are installed in the track at intervals of 1km (a little over half a mile). The information they contain relates to permanent speed restrictions which the APT driver must observe; through many of them he can travel faster than the ordinary train, and there are others which apply only to him. When engineering work imposes temporary speed restrictions the transponders can be 'blacked out' by covering them with metal covers and all traffic then obeys the limits displayed on lineside signs.

BR is currently working on an automatic train operating (ato) system known as BRATO in which signals to control the speed of the train are transmitted to it from conductors laid in the track in the form of long loops. The information received consists of the state of the signals, speed limits and track gradient. From this data duplicate computers in the train calculate its safe speed and control the traction equipment accordingly, taking into account the characteristics of the train itself. In this installation three microprocessors work in parallel and for the train to be allowed to proceed two must be in agreement. If the third 'dissents', it is isolated by the other two blowing a fuse and the train can carry on provided the two remaining in service continue to agree.

11 Passenger Rolling Stock

by Charles Long

In the early days of Nationalisation coaches built by BR generally reflected the later practice of the Grouped companies. The first Mk I coaches introduced in 1951 carried on, among other features already seen elsewhere, the large deep windows with sliding ventilators above which had been used by the LMSR since the 1930s. A load-carrying underframe supported an all-steel welded body. There was no insulation between outer and inner bodyside or roof panels; the floor was of multi-ply on steel framing, again without insulation. Windows were single-glazed. Steam heating was by radiant tubular heaters and lighting was at 24V dc with axle-driven generators. The standard body length of the Mk I vehicles was 64ft 6in, width 9ft 0in and tare weight originally about 32 tons, although later vehicles, mounted on 'Commonwealth' cast steel bogies, incorporating double-glazing, a measure of sound and thermal insulation and various other improvements were three tons or more heavier. All vans and some non-corridor coaches (the latter all now withdrawn from BR service) appeared on a shorter underframe, 56ft 11in long.

A particularly noteworthy feature of the Mk I construction period — which, so far as locomotive-hauled stock is concerned, lasted until the mid-1960s — is the number of different types of

Below: An early BR Mk I corridor composite (CK) coach in the original red-and-cream livery. There are four first class compartments and three second class. The coach is mounted on B1 type bogies, with leaf spring primary suspension. BR

'standard' vehicles produced. For example, even the basic main line second class coach came in four different layouts — either in side corridor or open saloon versions, each with three- or four-a-side seating — although all shared a basically similar bodyshell. No succeeding series of coaches has been produced in such a wide variety of types (see table).

In the next generation of rolling stock (Mk II) BR made various changes to improve the ride at speeds up to 90mile/h and to provide a passenger environment more in line with contemporary ideas on decor and amenities. Body and underframe were designed as an integral load-bearing structure, and this helped in keeping weight down to 32 tons in spite of various additions which otherwise would have added to it. The floor was redesigned with insulation between upper and lower panels, bodyside and roof cavities were filled with insulating materials, and there was pressure-ventilation with provision for heating from a steam or electric supply. Windows

were double-glazed. All second class coaches were saloons, an arrangement considered to allow more scope for comfortable seating with four seats across the width of the coach. Three-a-side compartments were retained for first class. All vehicles had a body length of 66ft.

The first Mk II coach was introduced in 1963. Series production began in 1966. Much attention was being given by industry and commerce at this time to improved lighting, taking advantage of the high luminous efficiency of the fluorescent tube. There had already been some experiments with fluorescent lighting operated on the normal carriage dc supply but here there was the problem that with a dc supply a fluorescent lamp tends to blacken at one end of the tube. The on/off switches were therefore arranged to reverse the polarity each time they were operated. It was soon possible to drop this inconvenient arrangement because semiconductor inverters enabled ac for the lamps to be provided from a dc system. At the same period the semiconductor power rectifier was reaching full development and so the pattern emerged of an axle-driven train-lighting alternator, a rectifier for battery charging and inverters between the battery and the fluorescent lamps.

Left: BR Mk I composite sleeper on the original B1 bogies. The coach is in the maroon livery of the 1957-65 period. BR

Below left: BR Mk I brake corridor first (BFK), mounted on cast steel 'Commonwealth' bogies with coil spring primary suspension. Brian Haresnape

Below: BR Mk I Post Office stowage van (POS), mounted on B5 heavy duty bogies with coil spring primary suspension. J. W. A. Brown

Top: BR Mk IIa open second (TSO), mounted on B4 bogies with coil spring primary suspension. BR

Above: BR Mk IIc open second (TSO), with 'wrap-round' wide end doors. BR

Top right: BR Mk IId open first (FO), with full air-conditioning. Note the absence of sliding opening panels above the main windows, which are tinted double-glazed units. BR

Mk II stock was fitted with improved luggage racks containing tungsten spotlight reading lamps recessed into them. Illumination of a book being read by a passenger was 10 lumens/sq ft compared with 2 lumens/sq ft in Mk I stock.

Further development of Mk II stock was seen in the Mk IIa vehicles of 1967, equipped with air brakes and dual heating. End vestibule connections were completely redesigned. Internally, timber and glazed corridor partitions were replaced by metal partitions and sliding doors, giving greater glass area and a more pleasing appearance.

Mk IIb was introduced in 1968, characterised externally by wide wrap-round doors while an altered layout in the second class open vehicle removed the centre vestibule and provided a toilet at each end of the coach.

By this time market research was showing a public demand for air-conditioning. Some of the Mk IIb coaches under construction in 1969 were fitted with a new ceiling incorporating ducting in readiness for installing air-conditioning at a later date. These were known as Mk IIc. The first coaches built with air-conditioning from the start were MkIId, and the first of these went into service on the Eastern Region between Kings Cross and Newcastle on 12 July 1971.

For compatibility with existing stock the same system of heating by feeding heated air into the coach below seat level was retained but the cooled air was supplied through overhead ducts from an air-conditioner on the underframe.

The advent of electric traction at 25kV ac enabled passenger coaches to be heated with a nominal 800V supply taken from a heating winding on the locomotive transformer. Rolling stock had to be dual-equipped so that when diesel-hauled it could be heated from the train heating boiler in the diesel locomotive. This was a temporary arrangement, and steps were soon taken to equip main line diesel locomotives with means of producing a train heating supply. At first the supply was generated as dc but later three-phase auxiliary alternators were fitted, although the supply to the train heating line was rectified so that the existing two-wire system could be used.

The Mk IId coach accepted either dc or single-phase ac from the

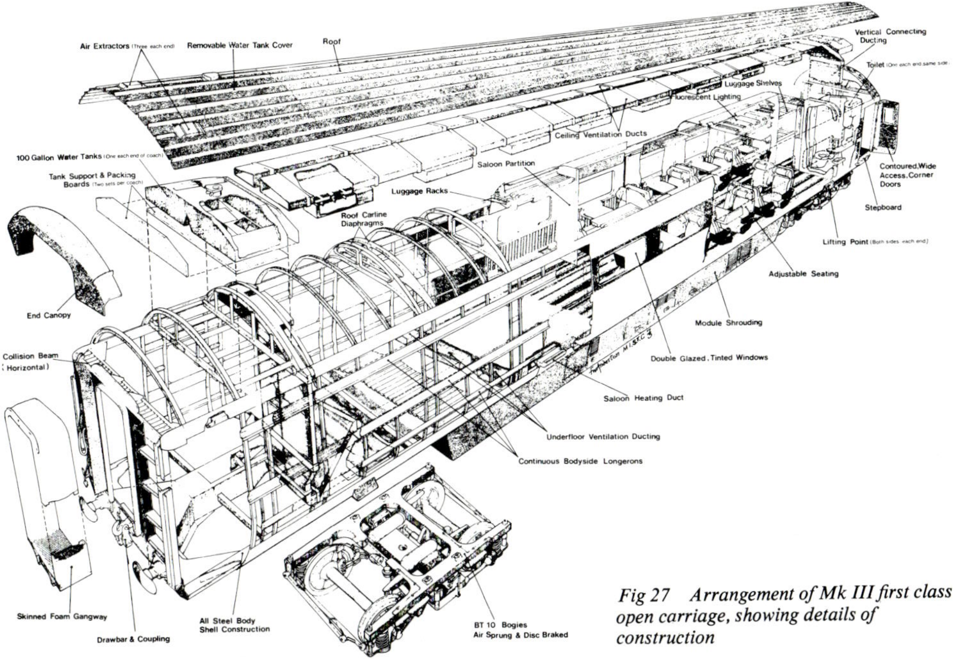

Fig 27 Arrangement of Mk III first class open carriage, showing details of construction

locomotive. This input supplied the coach heaters. It also powered a motor-alternator giving a local three-phase supply for the air-conditioner. 'Domestic' services, eg shaver sockets and toilet water heaters, were connected across one phase of the three-phase supply. A three-phase/dc rectifier provided for battery charging, fluorescent lighting via inverters, and the ventilating fan, which had to be able to run off the battery in case of a power failure. All coaches were equipped with public address, which was also a battery load.

After Mk IId, the IIe and IIf versions followed in quick succession, featuring an improved vestibule layout, modified air-conditioning and new Inter-City style seating. In the SO the seating was increased from 62 to 64, and in the BSO from 31 to 32. With the Mk IIe series the building of-side-corridor first class vehicles was finally abandoned.

The various Mk II versions have been followed by the Mk III coaches (Fig 27), now familiar both on locomotive-hauled services and on the High Speed Trains. All seating in Mk III stock is in open saloons. It is again fully air-conditioned and the supply arrangements are generally similar to MK IId but with the battery voltage increased from 28 to 110V. The HST coaches, however, are not compatible with the locomotive-hauled coaches, designated Mk IIIa, because they take their three-phase supply from the power cars instead of having their own alternators.

Below: Interior of Mk IId open first (FO). BR

Top: Mk III coaches under construction at BREL Derby Litchurch Lane Works. BR

Above: Mk III HST trailer restaurant unclassified buffet (TRUB), mounted on B10 bogies. The air-conditioning and other ancillary equipment is mounted in the underfloor shrouding between the bogies, and complete 'packages' are exchanged for maintenance purposes. BR

Internal doors are air-operated but the pneumatic actuators are controlled electrically by treadle switches under the mats.

The 75ft long Mk III coach is a highly sophisticated relatively lightweight (32 tons tare) vehicle which is anticipated to have a life of more than 30 years. The body is an integral all-welded mild steel structure, like all BR passenger coaches designed to withstand an end compression load of 200 tons. An identical bodyshell is used for both the 48-seat first class and 72-seat second class open type coaches so that, should business patterns change at some future date, interior layouts can be readily altered.

For the HST units three types of catering vehicle have been evolved, namely: a Trailer Restaurant Unclassed Kitchen (TRUK) with 23 seats of first class pattern; a Trailer Restaurant Buffet Second (TRSB) with 34 second class seats; and a Trailer Restaurant Unclassed Buffet with 17 seats of first class type. Normally the East Coast HST formations include both a TRUK to provide a full meal service and a TRSB for light refreshments, while Western Region (and the forthcoming Northwest-Southwest sets) have a single TRUB which incorporates a buffet bar similar to that of the TRSB but includes an enlarged kitchen area for the preparation of main meals. All three types are equipped with microwave ovens to speed the cooking of hot dishes.

Recently introduced on the West Coast main line is a locomotive-hauled version of the TRUB vehicle, classified RUB. These Mk III

Below: Close-up of 'Commonwealth' cast steel bogie used on late-series Mk I stock. A. Swain

Bottom: B4 bogie, used on most Mk II series coaches, and for rebogying Mk I vehicles. The B5 bogie is a heavy-duty variant. BR

cars are the first new general purpose catering vehicles to enter service for more than 10 years. In the meantime many Mk I cars have been refurbished and equipped with new bogies, but they have been hard-pressed and availability has suffered.

All sleepers at present in service are Mk I series cars, variously with 11 single-berth first class compartments, 11 two-berth second class compartments, or five first and six second class compartments. All have pressure ventilation. A new series of Mk III sleepers is due to enter service in the early 1980s. They will have convertible compartments with a fixed single berth for first class use and a second upper fold-down berth to produce a two-berth second class layout.

The design of diesel and electric multiple-unit vehicles has generally followed in the wake of contemporary locomotive-hauled stock although light-alloy body panels and components were used in some of BR's earliest dmus. The latest series of emus for inner suburban services are of distinctive clean-cut outline and feature air-operated double-leaf sliding doors.

Carriage bogie designs have been continuously developed to provide a comfortable ride at higher speeds. Suspension and springing are complex subjects but it is easy to visualise what is required of them. A bogie proceeding along the track makes constant side-to-side movements which have to be absorbed by the suspension before they reach the body. Track irregularities cause vertical movements of the axles and the body has to be isolated from these as well. The coach body usually rests on a transverse beam, or 'bolster', which is not a part of the bogie frame but is

Below: A Class 314 emu for the Argyle Line in Glasgow which links the suburban systems north and south of the River Clyde, hence the 'Trans-Clyde' brand name, replacing the former 'Clyderail'. BR

Fig 28 *Bogie of BR Mk III passenger vehicle*

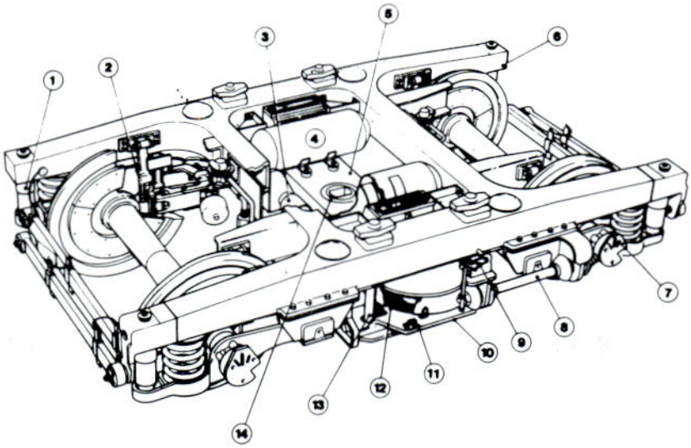

Key to Fig 28: **1**—*Primary damper.* **2**—*Disc brake.* **3**—*Lateral damper.* **4**—*Air reservoir.* **5**—*Bolster.* **6**—*Bogie frame.* **7**—*Wheel slide protection detector.* **8**—*Traction rod.* **9**—*Air suspension levelling valve.* **10**—*Spring plank.* **11**—*Air suspension indicator (shows if spring is deflated).* **12**—*Air spring.* **13**—*Swing link.* **14**—*Centre pivot.*

suspended from it with a small clearance at each end so that the frame can make sideways movements without striking the bolster. The suspension consists of swing links from the frame and connected at their lower ends by a 'spring plank' carrying coil springs on which the bolster rests.

The bolster must be restrained from moving appreciably in the fore-and-aft direction. This can be achieved by locating it between cross-members of the bogie frame with enough clearance to make it a sliding fit. Alternatively it can be anchored to the bogie frame by traction bars having rubber bushed mountings at each end to allow some freedom of lateral movement. These arrangements are known collectively as the secondary suspension. Recent practice has been to replace the coil springs of the secondary suspension with air springs. In the Class 313 emus there is no swing bolster, the air springs themselves accommodating relative sideways movements between bogie and body. The centre pivot is located by rubber-bushed traction links so that it can 'float' with the body movements. Mk III stock has air springs on a swing bolster (Fig 28) similar in principle to that already described.

The springing between the axleboxes and the bogie frame is the primary suspension. It has progressed from leaf springs to coil springs and to various arrangements of rubber bushed radius links which combine the functions of transmitting tractive effort while allowing vertical and some sideways movement of the axleboxes. Dampers are used in various combinations in both stages of vehicle suspension. In Mk III stock primary suspension of the axlebox is by an arm with a rubber bushed attachment to the bogie frame at its inner end and a coil spring between its outer end and the bogie frame.

BR Hauled Stock Type Codes

BCK	Brake Corridor Composite	Mk I
BFK	Brake Corridor First	Mk I, II, IIa, IIb, IIc, IId
BG	Brake, gangwayed	Mk I
BSK	Brake Corridor Second	Mk I, II
BSO	Brake Open Second	Mk I, II, IIa, IIc, IId, IIe, IIf
CK	Corridor Composite	Mk I
FK	Corridor First	Mk I, II, IIa, IIb, IIc, IId
FO	Open First	Mk I, IIc, IId, IIe, IIf, IIIa
RB	Buffet with Kitchen	Mk I
RB(K)	Kitchen/Buffet — 12 seats	Mk I
RBR	Refurbished Buffet	Mk I
RB(s)	RU rebuilt with Buffet	Mk I
RF	Restaurant First with Kitchen	Mk I
RG	Restaurant Griddle Car	Mk I
RK	Kitchen Car	Mk I
RKB	Kitchen/Buffet — no seats	Mk I
RMB	Open Second/small Buffet	Mk I
RSO	Rest Second — no kitchen	Mk I
RSS	Restaurant Self-Service	Mk IIf (experimental prototype)
RU	Unclassed Restaurant with Kitchen	Mk I
RUB	Unclassed Rest with Kitchen/Buffet	Mk IIIa
RU(B)	RU rebuilt with serving area	Mk I
SK	Corridor Second	Mk I
SO	Open Second — other than 62/64 seats	Mk I, II
TSO	Tourist Open Second — 62/64 seats (72 seats Mk IIIa)	Mk I, II, IIa, IIb, IIc, IId, IIe, IIf, IIIa

Sleeping cars, Post Office and other special-purpose vehicles are not shown in the above list. Multiple-unit vehicles use similar codes with the addition of the following letters used as a prefix: B=Battery; D=Driving; M=Motor; T=Trailer. The distinction between open and corridor stock is also ignored. Eg: BDTC=Battery Driving Trailer Composite; DMBF=Driving Motor Brake First; TS=Trailer Second.

12 Freight Services and Rolling Stock

Reminiscences of the past still cling to the railway image. Sometimes they can be turned to good account, such as nostalgia for the steam locomotive, which has brought in useful revenue from special excursions with steam haulage for part of the itinerary as the high point. The fact that steam traction has gone is accepted, albeit with regret, by all who take part. Another change is less well understood, and one still hears it asked, 'where have all the goods trains gone?'. What the speaker has in mind is the train of general merchandise, its miscellaneous assortment of wagons travelling from yard to yard on the way to their destination, some of them probably ending their journey in a local freight trip calling at all stations and discharging its load in some of the many goods sheds once so much a part of the railway scene.

This kind of freight operation belonged to the days when the railways had the obligations of common carriers and had to accept all loads offered to them. It was an obligation difficult to discharge efficiently, although when the railways had their own cartage fleets good progress was made with schemes for combined rail and road haulage which helped both the customer with quicker deliveries and the railways by more effective use of their resources. But these

Below: A block train of two-tier Cartic wagons conveying cars to distributors. BR

Above: A Freightliner train on the West Coast main line. BR

improvements were not enough to offset operating losses, and the Transport Act of 1968 set up the National Freight Corporation to take over the carriage of small consignments, using the road vehicles of National Carriers Ltd (NCL), many of them previously railway-owned. This is the situation today. NCL may use rail for part of a journey if full wagonloads can be made up but carriage is primarily by road. Relieved from its common carrier obligation, British Rail is now free to concentrate on traffic which it can work profitably. In 1978 it carried 171 million tons and, after years of Government support, reached the break-even point in this side of its business.

Today some 80% of the freight carried on British Rail moves in full trainloads, the remaining 20% being wagonload traffic. Only 10 years ago the proportions were approximately reversed. The change has come about naturally in the process of matching railway potential to the requirements of industry.

Coal is still the bread and butter of the railway freight business. It is a bulk traffic moving in a way that is attractive from the operating viewpoint, for example in merry-go-round (mgr) trains running direct from colliery to power station. In 1978 coal and coke by rail totalled 94 million tonnes of which 61 million tons were for power generation. The total has been remaining steady in spite of a fall in the tonnage of coal for the domestic consumer as further smokeless zones are created and there is a continuing trend to forms of home heating which involve less housework than the coal fire or solid fuel boiler. Domestic coal is sent from the pits to coal concentration depots throughout the country, from which it is collected by local merchants. The rail haul may be direct from colliery to depot, or trains may run to a yard where they are split up and several depots are served by local trips.

Iron, steel and ores are other traffics conveyed in bulk, and still second in volume to coal. Today new traffics are being won to supplement the traditional ones, some of them less subject to economic fluctuations. An unusual example is refuse disposal, which is a permanent requirement of local authorities. With the increasing use of materials, which cannot be burned, there is a growing need to shift refuse often over considerable distances to sites where it can be buried. In 1977 BR began conveying refuse for the Greater London Council from several London boroughs to a landfill site at Appleford, Oxfordshire. The trains operate from a GLC compaction depot on the site of the former Brentford Town goods depot, conveying the refuse in block trainloads of special containers. A year later a similar operation was inaugurated for the GLC between Cricklewood and Stewartby, Bedfordshire. Refuse disposal is a new market and a growing one.

Changing circumstances are creating another growth area for freight by rail. In some parts of the country sources of earths and stones used in the production of building and road making materials are becoming worked out and suppliers find it necessary to go further afield. Business in conveying these materials is increasing. In 1978 BR carried 15.1 million tons and the prospects remain good. Trainloads of cement, with their distinctive types of wagon, must be among the most familiar aspects of modern railway freight operation to the observer and are another sign of activity in the same area. Sometimes there is local concern at the revival of traffic at a terminal which has been unused for a long time but objectors

Below: Vans used in the Speedlink network are designed for convenient loading and unloading by mechanical handling equipment. BR

usually soon see the force of the argument that such operations are less detrimental to the environment than the more random traffic patterns when materials are conveyed by road transport throughout.

Agriculture is a source of bulk traffic such as grain from farms to granary, and seed potatoes from Scotland to large growers all over the country. The products of the chemical industry travel partly in bulk and partly as packaged goods. Rail transport is mainly of the bulk products, and here the good safety record of the railways and the controlled conditions of train movement are points appreciated by customers.

The railways compete very strongly with pipelines and coastal shipping in the carriage of petroleum products, most of the rail movement being from refineries to oil terminals. Carriage is mostly in privately-owned wagons, which is an advantage to the railway because it would be difficult to keep these specialised vehicles sufficiently employed between their scheduled journeys to justify the cost of building them for BR ownership.

The motor industry is a source of bulk traffic such as the conveyance of components and car bodies between plants. Also bulk deliveries of completed vehicles on behalf of the delivery agents form an important part of the railway contribution in this field.

The industries considered so far are able to forward traffic in trainloads moving between private sidings. Its variety is great and new contracts are frequently announced in the railway press. A typical example is the 10 year contract signed in April 1978 for conveying limestone aggregate from the Foster Yeoman quarry at Merehead, Somerset, to the company's rail-served terminal at

Below: FBT6 bogie for bogie steel carrier wagons. BREL

Acton, one of four supplying the Home Counties north of the Thames. A double-headed train with a payload of 1,400 tonnes in 37 high-capacity hopper wagons is run on four days a week. Since the Transport Act of 1974 Government grants have been made to assist companies establishing or improving their rail connections where environmental advantages are gained, thus adding considerably to the attraction of using rail services.

Many companies which would not be in a position to forward freight in trainloads, but have been despatching products by road in lorry-loads, are now using BR's network of Speedlink air-braked express freight trains running between railheads in the principal industrial centres. The trains are formed of high-capacity wagons able to run at speeds up to 75mile/h. Wagons for loading are delivered to the customer's siding or nearest rail terminal. They then join others in the appropriate Speedlink service and on arrival at destination are either delivered to the consignee's private siding or made available for unloading at the terminal. Most Speedlink trains run overnight and provide next morning delivery. Details of wagons and loads on every train, Speedlink or other service are transmitted to destination terminals as soon as a train departs, as part of the TOPS computerised monitoring system.

The TOPS computers at BRB headquarters in London store the basic details of every wagon and van. Day-to-day information, for example where a wagon is at any time, its load, destination, service by which travelling and so on, is transmitted to the computer centre from 138 Area Freight Centres and associated with the fixed information held in the store. Any query regarding a wagon can be answered by transmitting a request to the computer from terminal equipment at the Centre or from a BR manager's office. Customers can also have direct access to the computer from their own Telex installations. TOPS is a time-sharing system, and replies are printed out on the terminal printer or customer's Telex machine with only a few seconds delay, just as if the computer was in the same building as the enquirer and working exclusively for him.

TOPS has generated a confidence in rail freight that was never achieved so fully in the days when queries had to be dealt with by numerous telephone calls and consultation of written records, a slow and often unsatisfactory process. But this is only one side of the service, although sometimes the one most appreciated by the customer. The system also monitors the whole transit operation and provides much valuable data which management can use in maintaining and improving the efficiency of the service. When a customer requests a wagon through his Area Freight Centre, TOPS allocates one of suitable type that is conveniently located. Its progress to destination is followed step by step, and after it is unloaded the computer assigns a new job for it, selecting one that will enable it to be loaded again and in revenue-earning service with the minimum of empty running.

Speedlink services now run to the train ferry ports of Dover and Harwich and TOPS follows the wagons until they reach Dunkerque or Zeebrugge, where they come under the control of the Continental railways.

With the present types of freight traffic flow on British Railways it has been possible to reduce the number of freight terminals from some 5,000 in 1962 to just over 400. Trainload working has reduced the need for marshalling yards and 186 marshalling facilities now meet the requirements, while early in 1979 the number of private sidings had reached 1,850. Proposals have been made to planning authorities for the development of 'freight complexes' with rail/road transhipment facilities and warehousing, sited conveniently for local distribution and access to trunk roads.

Below: The Y25C bogie being fitted to existing bogie bolster wagons which have been refurbished and equipped with air brakes. BREL

The services mentioned so far are siding-to-siding or siding-to-terminal. Door-to-door transport, usually combining trunk haulage by rail with road collection and delivery, is the special province of Freightliners Limited, the container-carrying organisation which is a wholly owned subsidiary of BR. Freightliners Limited remains an independent company continuing to own its containers, vehicles and 25 out of the 36 terminals it serves. The company employs 600 road vehicles, predominantly used for collection and delivery of containers but sometimes moving loads by road throughout in circumstances where an economic road/rail service cannot be provided. There are also some composite Speedlink/Freightliner trains on services where it would not be economic to run a complete Freightliner. New sources of traffic are continuously sought and new opportunities sought for the expansion of containerised movements. One example is the opentop container for carrying Fletton bricks, introduced in 1973 for traffic from the London Brick Company's works at Fletton, near Stewartby, Beds, to the company's distribution centres. The contract was renewed for a further five-year term in 1978. Two trains called 'Fletliners' run daily from the works, one to London Kings Cross and the other to Manchester and Liverpool. About 50% of Freightliner Limited's traffic is in moving exports to and from the ports. Extra facilities have been developed at Tilbury and new capacity to meet growing demand has been provided at Felixstowe, Liverpool and Greenock.

In variety of articles handled and multiplicity of customers perhaps the closest equivalent to the old railway 'sundries' traffic is the Rail Express Parcels service, although this traffic is conveyed entirely by passenger trains or by special parcels trains running at passenger train speeds. The Post Office is the largest single customer, with many passenger and parcels trains carrying letter mail and/or parcels post. The most important development recently has been the Red Star parcels service conveying parcels by scheduled express passenger trains. The sender can specify the train by which he wishes his parcel to travel and knows the time at which it will arrive at the destination station. Normally the addressee can collect it 30min after the arrival time of the train. Red Star parcels are carried on High Speed Trains on routes where these are running and extra space has been made available for them to meet the demand.

Red Star service is particularly attractive to business and

Above: Two-axle plate wagon, Type SPA. BREL

industry, and by the introduction of the complementary City Link road collection and delivery service now provides door-to-door transits. City Link vans also bridge the gap between trains where there is no through service, conveying parcels between London termini, for example, or between stations in other cities where transfer is necessary. City Link has offices in 20 main centres supported by agents in over 150 cities and towns. In collaboration with Red Star and British Airways it provides the Jetlink service for parcels to the United States by Concorde flights, conveying them between the London termini and Heathrow Airport. A package collected from an office in Newcastle at close of business on one day can be in New York at 10.00 local time the next morning.

The present pattern of freight services on BR results in large numbers of privately-owned wagons being used to form 'company' trains conveying siding-to-siding traffic. Designs for these wagons must be vetted, approved and registered by British Rail CM&EE, BRB and construction is supervised throughout by BR inspection engineers. BREL itself builds for the private owner in its own works.

All new construction since 1966/67 has been air-braked. All wagons carry a three-letter code which is used to describe them in TOPS documents and procedures. An example is the 102-tonne bogie steel carrier, BBA of which some 800 are in traffic. The vehicle is mounted on FBT6 bogies with coil spring primary suspension and is disc-braked on all wheels. This is a flat open wagon with raised ends for all kinds of steel traffic. Sockets are provided for fitting stanchions at variable intervals. With a length over headstocks of 15,240mm (50ft) the vehicle has a carrying capacity of 73 tonnes. A similar vehicle, BAB/BAA measures 12,193mm (40ft) over headstocks but overall height from rail level to the top of the end bulkheads is some 9ft as compared with 8ft and the carrying capacity 77 tonnes.

A very large number of existing bogie bolster wagons originally without continuous brakes are being refurbished and air-braked, and fitted with new Y25C bogies with 20-tonne axleload. Later conversions in the series have been given disc brakes in place of the original brake blocks. These wagons are coded BDA. Gross laden weight is 80 tonnes and carrying capacity 57 tonnes.

Some 1,500 two-axle plate wagons of 46 tonnes gross laden weight are being built, designated SPA (steel plate air). The latest design has a tapered leaf spring suspension described as a friction controlled parabolic spring, and this is now being fitted to all new builds of two-axle wagons. As seen in an accompanying illustration, the leaves are in contact at ends and centre only, and the spring is a two-stage spring, the bottom spring only coming into play in full load conditions. With this arrangement the vertical ride is improved compared with conventional leaf springs. The wheelbase of 6,320mm (20ft 9in) is now usual for two-axle wagons unless there is a special reason for a shorter one. Maximum permitted speeds are 60mile/h at 46 tonnes gross laden weight and 75mile/h at 41 tonnes. Disc brakes and hand brakes are fitted.

The hopper wagon illustrated is the HAA hopper coal wagon of 32.5 tonnes capacity, and in this example is fitted with a canopy. Introduced originally for conveying pulverised coal to power stations in mgr trains, these vehicles and derivatives have later found wider use for other traffics. Mechanical discharge gear is fitted, acting in cooperation with trackside equipment at unloading points, but an air-operated system for opening the hopper doors at places not so equipped has been developed recently and a prototype exists. Air is taken from the train brakepipe and stored in a reservoir

Below: The friction-controlled parabolic spring suspension which is fitted to all new builds of two-axle wagons. BREL

on the wagon so that the doors can be opened pneumatically when the wagon is uncoupled from a train. Manual operation is also provided and the design of the mechanism is such that less effort is required than for working the previous type of mechanical gear. Maximum loaded speed for these wagons when introduced was 45mile/h but with disc braking and improved suspension this is being raised to 60mile/h subject to satisfactory trials. There is one disc brake on each axle, fitted at opposite corners of the wagon.

To all with memories of the railways in the early years of Nationalisation one of the striking aspects of the modern scene is the long wheelbase van which has succeeded the short box wagon familiar for so long. For use in today's express freight services, vans must be suitable for running at speeds up to 75mile/h. The latest design is the VDA vehicle of 40 tonnes glw and a carrying capacity of 26.5 tonnes. Length over headstocks is 10,210mm (33ft 6in) and the wheelbase is the 6,320mm mentioned above as becoming standard for two-axle stock. There are three pairs of doors in each side, the centre one sliding and the end doors hinged. Research into suspension systems for high-speed freight vehicles has been pursued

Below: Type HAA hopper wagon with canopy. BREL

Right: Type VDA van as used on Speedlink services, with centre sliding and end hinged doors. BREL

Below right: Taperlite suspension fitted to a VDA van. BREL

for some years. One of its products is the Taperlite suspension fitted to 100 vehicles of the VDA series. The vertical suspension at each axlebox consists of two sets of springs (see illustration) — a two-leaf tapered spring and two groups of coil springs. Under light loads both groups work together in series. As load increases the coil springs are blocked out by stops and the leaf springs alone take over the suspension, providing a higher degree of stiffness. The two components are connected by swing links, which can be seen in the illustration together with the longitudinal rod from a bracket on the axlebox to the suspension structure which anchors the axlebox in the fore and aft direction but also allows some transverse

movement. Dampers to control vertical and transverse movements are fitted at each axlebox. In the illustration the vertical damper is seen immediately above the box, with one end of the lateral damper visible immediately to its left.

Earlier series of vans, VBA and VCA, have sliding doors only and are restricted to 60mile/h at full load. Altogether BREL has built some 1,400 vans of modern designs for BR Speedlink wagonload services, and the airbraked open vehicles already referred to are also used in these trains when appropriate.

Two types of vehicle have been built for car-carrying in Motorail trains. These are Carflats, converted from former passenger stock, and the two-tier Cartics. A Cartic consists of four articulated units carried on five two-axle bogies, the ends of two adjacent units resting on each inner bogie.

Freightliners began operations before the formation of BREL in 1970 but the present BREL works were building Freightliner vehicles from the beginning and these were, in fact, their first two-piped air-braked products. Some 2,000 are now in service. The most numerous are the 52ft Freightliner 'inners', Class FFA, for carrying containers in various combinations. A Freightliner train consists of two 'outers' with standard buffing and draw-gear and a variable number of 'inners'. Other types are the 40ft and 60ft 'Lowliners'.

Below: Sea Freightliner 1 *container ship for services between Harwich Parkeston Quay and the Netherlands.*